LEADERSHIP
IN A
TIME OF CRISIS

THE WAY FORWARD
IN A CHANGED WORLD

Compiled by
Marshall Goldsmith and Scott Osman

RosettaBooks®
NEW YORK 2020

Dedicated to the workers who are showing up every day during
the crisis, demonstrating leadership and commitment.

Leadership in a Time of Crisis

First edition published 2020 by RosettaBooks

Cover design by Lee Iley

ISBN-13 (print): 978-0-7953-5294-2
ISBN-13 (ebook): 978-0-7953-5293-5

Library of Congress Control Number: 2020937401

RosettaBooks®

www.RosettaBooks.com
Printed in the United States of America

MARSHALL GOLDSMITH
1CO
COACHES

CONTENTS

FOREWORD

Quality, character, courage, and "beyond the call" describe those who respond to these unexpected national pandemics—the frontline responders and their families.

Nonprofit organizations are particularly challenged, as they work with communities whose needs have not changed, while the way we work in the world has been turned upside-down in many ways. It is inspiring to see how they are reinventing themselves. University students and faculty are working hard to adapt to and excel in exceptionally speedy transitions to remote environments. Corporations are working to educate their staff on ways to be technologically connected. Leaders in all sectors are shifting into overdrive.

It has been interesting to hear from many colleagues, collaborators, and leaders who have shared with us their own challenges and digital opportunities during this uncertain time.

Our leadership work at the Frances Hesselbein Leadership Forum, housed in the Graduate School of Public and International Affairs at the University of Pittsburgh, fosters the development of values-based leadership: developing leaders of character and competence; providing dynamic global mentorship, training and service opportunities; and engaging, informing and enhancing the leadership journey of incoming generations of leaders.

In March 2020 we surveyed leaders from all levels, in every sector. Respondents cited their **top three** leadership challenges as:

1. Maintaining work goals and future planning
2. Financial and funding issues
3. Lack of personal connection

Liz Wiseman's contribution "Leading in the Dark" advises: "Rather than waiting for information or pretending you've got it figured out, let your people know what you don't know." And in "Unleash Your Superpower and Focus on Who You Want to BE," Ekpedeme "Pamay" M. Bassey writes: "In times of adversity, one of the best things you can do as a leader is to stay focused on the truth that learning is your superpower. The best way to address any challenge is to learn your way through it."

Despite these challenges, leaders attested to pleasant surprises in their remote working environments: the opportunity to think, read, study, and learn new things; an improved environment related to reduced national and global pollution; authentic availability and engagement; and enhanced collaboration.

One response was particularly significant: "I have learned how committed, ethical, and trustworthy my team is."

Adrian Gostick and Chester Elton, experts in gratitude, have some great wisdom in their piece, "How to Remove Fear from Your Work Culture." They write: "During tough times, it's more important than ever to be honest and transparent. When employees know their managers are seeking better ways during tough times, and are encouraging them to practice the same, it builds trust and a larger culture of optimism." In "Three Strategies to Keep Team Members Calm and Productive under Heightened Stress," Sharon Melnick offers the following: "Optimism paints a positive picture of the future you see, implying there's something each person can do to help achieve success. Realism sets the expectation that there will be discomfort and challenges, which can be adapted to and overcome."

In our survey, we asked our customers which leadership topics they most wanted to explore more deeply? Where should we focus our leadership offerings? They responded:

1. Mindfulness
2. Leading in a crisis
3. Self-care

Elsewhere in this book, in "Finding Our Finest Hour," Laura Gassner Otting writes "opportunities to be of service are plentiful." Shoma Heyden in the "The Importance of CEO Self-Care during Prolonged Crises" reminds us that: "One thing utterly in a CEO's control right now is showing up in their absolute best condition to perform for themselves, their people, and the communities in which they operate."

Taken together, these articles provide a blueprint on how leaders might reframe their current reality, how they might consider this crisis a unique time of opportunity. In the end, leadership is a matter of how to be, not how to do.

As Ayse Birsel notes in "Breaking and Rebuilding," "The times call for transformation, but none of us can afford to let it just happen. Rather, here's how we can do it intentionally." Read on, dear leaders.

Frances Hesselbein
New York City
April 2020

INTRODUCTION: THE WAY FORWARD IN A CHANGED WORLD

After attending Ayse Birsel's transformative "Design the Life You Love" workshop, I (Marshall) was inspired to start the 100 Coaches Pay It Forward project. The idea was to teach everything I know to fifteen highly motivated coaches and leaders—for free—on the sole condition that they, too, adopt fifteen people in their turn and pay it forward. It was the beginning of a ripple effect based on my commitment to helping talented people achieve the most with their abilities.

A simple video invitation on LinkedIn has now been answered by over 18,000 people, and I (Scott) joined as CEO to explore the potential of the 100 Coaches project. Since then, we have adopted over 250 amazing people and are profoundly grateful to everyone who is supporting and involved in this wonderful program. Our members are among the top executive coaches, leadership thinkers, and leaders in the world.

In early March 2020, as the present crisis was unfolding, our group began meeting daily to discuss the developments and repercussions of current events. We heard from global leaders around the world, from leadership thinkers who were beginning to think about the impact on all aspects of our global economy. We considered the pandemic's ramifications on people, on the healthcare system, on local, national, and global economies, and on our businesses. Gathering these insights is a work in progress and constitutes a view from the end of the beginning of the storm. We know that the business world will never be the same again.

While our understanding of the crisis is imperfect, we recognize that leaders are looking for the best guidance and direction they can find. We invited a selection of the 100 Coaches to share one insight that could most help leaders during this time of unprecedented crisis. Time will tell how accurate we are.

The ambition of the 100 Coaches is to reinforce the recognition that by creating value for all stakeholders the best leaders create more sustainable value for their shareholders as well. We are committed to bringing the best talent and thinking to the best leaders and future leaders. Each of the 100 Coaches, and the writers of this book, believe that by supporting the growth and development of leaders in all areas, we can create more value in the companies we serve and better lives for the people with whom we work and the communities in which we live.

This book offers a wide range of thought. We trust that these pages will be helpful to you as you work to bring out the best in yourself and the best in others. Take a deep breath. Take action. Keep moving forward.

Life is good.

Marshall and Scott

Dr. Marshall Goldsmith is a member of the Thinkers 50 Hall of Fame. He is the only two-time Thinkers 50 #1 Leadership Thinker in the World. He has been ranked as the World's #1 Executive Coach and Top Ten Business Thinker for eight years. Marshall was chosen as the inaugural winner of the Lifetime Award for Leadership by the Harvard Institute of Coaching. He is the author or editor of forty-one books, which have sold over 2.5 million copies, been translated into thirty-two languages and become listed bestsellers in twelve countries. His books, *Triggers* and *What Got You Here Won't Get You There*, were both recognized by Amazon as being in the top 100 books ever written in their field. Marshall's other professional acknowledgments include: Global Gurus—the inaugural Corps D 'Elite Award for Lifetime Contribution in Leadership and Coaching, *Harvard Business Review*—World's #1 Leadership Thinker, Institute for Management Studies—Lifetime Achievement Award for Leadership Education, American Management Association—50 great thinkers and leaders who have influenced the field of management over the past eighty years and *BusinessWeek*—50 great leaders in America.

Scott Osman is the founding CEO of Marshall Goldsmith 100 Coaches. An accomplished senior executive with more than thirty years of experience in leadership positions for companies in technology, strategy, and business development, and is well known as a thought leader in the area of purpose strategy. Scott has founded, grown, evolved, and marketed a diverse group of companies including serving as president of Doublespace, a digital agency located in New York City, and as Global Director at Landor Associates. Scott is based in New York and a graduate of Dartmouth College and has an MBA from NYU Stern.

Marshall Goldsmith 100 Coaches is an organization that brings together many of the world's leading executive coaches, top business thinkers, and best leaders with the common purpose of making good executives better. The organization offers services, events, online courses, and other opportunities to inspire, develop, and energize leaders for the future. For more information, visit 100CoachesConsulting.com.

HOW TO CREATE A SYMPHONY OF INCLUSION IN A COVID-19 WORLD

Oshoke Abalu

Smallpox had been ravaging the world for thousands of years before a vaccine was discovered in 1796. It was then that Dr. Edward Jenner shared his observations that dairy workers who had been infected with cowpox did not seem to catch smallpox. His inclusive perspective led to the solution for our lifelong protection from smallpox, a contribution that humans continue to benefit from today.

As French Renaissance philosopher Michel de Montaigne observed: "There never were in the world two opinions alike, any more than two hairs or two grains. Their most universal quality is diversity."

We must not miss our privilege to unlearn stale patterns and confront limited narratives in these uncertain times. Diversity and inclusion programs have an unprecedented opportunity to champion a "we" agenda and serve the reunion of humanity. If we do not act out of intention, we may compromise the future. It demands our attention over our afterthoughts, our empathy over our assumptions, and a dignified re-perception of each other, as equal and unique expressions of humanity in cooperation for the connectivity of our whole.

Each of us is called to step up and into the light of our privilege to participate in a cohesive narrative of our greatest collective intention: Symphony. This is a true north that serves our humanity and inspires the resuscitation of our individual and organizational latent superpowers—our individual complexities and idiosyncrasies—as our greatest resource in preparing for a future that we do not know. "Today, we have the necessary technologies to address all human problems," Indian yogi and author Sadhguru says. "All that is missing is an inclusive consciousness."

So, how do we get started? It is simple, and we can all play within these three "mindful keys" to practicing symphony in our organizations and communities.

Be aware of your language and its impact on inclusion

Words are the most powerful force available to humanity, and during these times we are tasked to confront the words we're using when talking about diversity and inclusion. We are also called to remember that inclusion is not about making room in the portrait for that "diverse other," but observing instead that the portrait is incomplete without "all of us" and adjusting the resonance of our invitation accordingly.

"Diversity" translates to discord in a range of different elements. "Symphony" translates to cooperation in a range of different elements. Diversity is a memory of an old world we've left behind. Symphony is a vision of a new world we are building. Together.

Reflect and refocus

Change your focus from what job you have and what role you play to ask yourself who you help and what problems you solve.

Symphony requires the hard work of a mindful refocus from the organizational indifference of meeting diversity targets to a new language of showing up for freedom for all.

"Work is love made visible," Kahlil Gibran said. "For if you bake bread with indifference, you bake a bitter bread that feeds but half man's hunger. . . . And if you sing though as angels, and love not the singing, you muffle man's ears to the voices of the day and the voices of the night."

Recalibrate

Build your awareness to perceive inclusion, not as a charitable opportunity, but rather as a necessary part of every organization's innovation and relevance.

The broader the scale of inclusion, the more powerful an organization's influence and impact will be during this new age, where workplaces are evolving from physical spaces to states of mind.

Inclusion is a precursor to an organization's edge, and its adaptive capacity to deal with rapid change. Like never before, the effectiveness and uniqueness of the perception of an organization's people have become its crown jewels in today's new digital economy.

Inclusion is no longer affirmative action. It is necessary action.

Oshoke Abalu is cofounder of Love & Magic Company, a techforward, inclusive-innovation consultancy, focused on transforming start-ups and corporations alike into what they call "beloved" organizations. Their tagline is the Khalil Gibran quote "Work is love made visible."

DETERMINE THE ROLES THE BOARD SHOULD TAKE

Asheesh Advani

During a crisis, what is the role of the board and what is the role of the CEO? With clarity about these roles, leaders can move quickly to address unexpected challenges or to capitalize on unexpected opportunities during a crisis. On the flip side, organizations will stumble or fail if there is confusion in the delegated authorities of senior management or fuzziness about the risk profile of the board.

Over the past two decades, I have served on about twenty-five boards, each with its own culture. I lived through the 2008–2010 financial crisis and dealt with complex board dynamics that included disputes between board members with different time horizons and risk profiles. In my current capacity of CEO of JA Worldwide since 2015, I serve on seven boards across the Junior Achievement network. The relationships among board members and between the CEO and the board becomes critical during the rush to deal with the ripple effects of any crisis.

As with most organizations, the COVID-19 crisis has had a significant impact on JA Worldwide and the entire JA network. Our organization delivered programs in entrepreneurship, financial literacy, and work readiness programs to over twelve million youth in schools across the world in over 100 countries. Our programs are free for students and funded by philanthropy. As the pandemic has spread, schools have closed in over 130 countries and philanthropy has halted or slowed. Even the best crisis management plans did not anticipate such a unique set of circumstances at the local, national, and global levels.

There are decades when nothing happens, and there are weeks where decades happen

Over the past few weeks, I have witnessed the resilience of JA's national leaders accelerate our digital transformation. First, in China, our team managed youth programs using Zoom and WeChat for students in Wuhan and other parts of the country. Then, in Italy and Spain, JA events for high school kids went virtual using Microsoft Teams and other online collaboration tools. In the United States, Israel, India, United Kingdom, Canada, and many other countries, JA staff is innovating at a rapid rate to thrive in this changed market environment. JA's global headquarters team has collected all these local, national, and regional innovations under a unifying brand umbrella, #KeepLearning, and online at jaworldwide.org/keeplearning.

I have focused on communicating a simple-to-understand vision for what our organization will look like in two years. The JA network will have developed one of the largest collections of digital education assets in the world, spreading across more than 100 countries. The digital transformation of the Junior Achievement network, while part of our 2020–22 strategic plan, has been accelerated with an urgency that we would have been hard-pressed to create in any other way.

Never let a crisis go to waste: What role do board members have in a crisis?

JA has over 6,000 board members throughout the world, organized as a network of teams (with over 300 separate legal entities, connected by a set of common operating agreements) at the local, national, regional, and global levels. (JA's networked organizational structure enables us to balance global benefits—such as funding, standards, shared IP, technology, brand—with local solutions, since school systems are usually managed at the local level with national and global guidelines. In each case, the role of the board and the role of the CEO is modified at the time of crisis.) Urgent questions about the financial sustainability of the organization, the process of reviewing/adapting budgets, and the viability of making investments in digital programs needed to be addressed rapidly and strategically with the consensus of the board and senior management.

To help inform these decisions, here are a few guidelines for board members to understand their role during the time of a crisis. These guidelines are adapted from two sources: a document prepared by US law firm Wachtell Lipton, and a document prepared by Jordi Canals from IESE Business School in Spain. They also reflect my own experience.

1. Ask the CEO to update the enterprise risk framework so that there is a shared understanding of new risks and management's strategy for mitigating these risks.
2. Review the sustainability and viability of the enterprise.
3. Request that management make appropriate changes to the approved budget and strategic plan to ensure the sustainability and viability of the enterprise.
4. Ensure that management has prioritized the health, well-being, and safety of employees, other stakeholders, and the public.
5. Review and stress-test all indebtedness, cash position, and liquidity needs of the enterprise with a time horizon of at least six months.
6. Participate in communications plans with internal and external groups, providing support to the CEO and senior management.
7. Support opportunities that arise from the crisis, including transactions with other enterprises and the acceleration of digital initiatives.
8. Reassess compensation plans, dividend plans, and large contracts with third parties as part of the budget review exercise.

9. Provide time and space to the CEO and senior management to have the necessary resources required to communicate, reprioritize, and adjust the organization to the new reality.
10. Maintain decorum and respect among board members and management, which are sometimes strained during crises.

Generally, the board must remember that it does not manage the enterprise and that its role is to support the CEO and senior management during the crisis. The quality of the communication between the CEO and the board will play a large part in strengthening or weakening the reputation of the enterprise after the crisis. The ability to seek opportunities that arise from the crisis—such as an accelerated digital transformation, strategic transactions, and organizational realignment—is possible only once the board and CEO are aligned on sustainability, viability, and risk management during the crisis.

Asheesh Advani is the president and CEO of JA (Junior Achievement) Worldwide, one of the largest NGOs in the world dedicated to preparing youth for the future of work. He is also an accomplished technology entrepreneur and serves on boards of corporations, venture-backed startups, and nonprofits. Advani is a graduate of the Wharton School and Oxford University.

UNLEASH YOUR SUPERPOWER, AND FOCUS ON WHO YOU WANT TO BE

Ekpedeme "Pamay" M. Bassey

Take a moment to think about the people you admire for their substantial impact and for their ability to deliver excellence consistently—no matter what the context or the circumstance. Whether that person is a mentor, a favorite manager, or an admired world leader, they probably have at least one thing in common: they are voracious learners. Exceptional leaders are everyday learners. They are lifelong learners. Or, to use a phrase made popular by internet entrepreneur and venture capitalist Reid Hoffman, they are "infinite learners": that is, they have an ability to learn constantly and to learn quickly.

In times of adversity, one of the best things you can do as a leader is to stay focused on the truth that *learning is your superpower.* The best way to address any challenge is to *learn your way through it.* In difficult times, you will be called upon to be your best self. Unleash your superpower to help yourself and to help those who depend on you. Maintain a laser focus on who you want to *BE* in the midst of the storm, and use that to direct your learning.

What are good ways to *BE* in uncertain times? Consider this:

- Be relentless.
- Be selective.
- Be uncompromising.

Let me explain.

Be relentless

Be relentless in your pursuit of any knowledge that can help you, your loved ones, your team, your community. Make time to reflect regularly on what you are learning. Use what you learn to address the challenge at hand—to make the next right decision, to take the next step, to communicate to your stakeholders. Even and especially if the crisis is too big to be tackled as a whole, be transparent about what you know, what you don't know, and share what you determine to be of value. Make it clear that you are doing everything you can to learn what you *need* to learn to make choices that will move things forward into whatever the "new normal" will be. Encourage others to do the same.

The beauty of having a learning practice is that you are constantly taking in new ideas and new perspectives, turning them over in your mind, making connections, and finding places and spaces where that information applies to your current situation.

Learn from those who have gone before you who have faced similar challenges. And never stop trying to take the pieces and parts of what may, at first glance, seem unrelated, but when synthesized can reveal innovative ideas about how to address the trial at hand. Leave no stone unturned as you seek your breakthrough.

Even if you find, in the midst of a crisis, that you have yet to establish a regular learning practice, it is never too late. As the late tennis legend and activist Arthur Ashe famously said, "Start where you are. Use what you have. Do what you can." Make a commitment to take the time to learn something new every day, even if it is just for a few minutes—read an article, listen to a podcast, have a conversation, research related topics. Persistently seek out whatever viewpoints you need to help you to make a plan, execute that plan, adjust the plan, and forge ahead.

Be selective

Decide to rely on trusted sources, and do your best to ignore the rest. During crises, life often changes in ways that most of us could not have anticipated. Things often move at a speed that require a great deal of resilience, courage, faith, and whatever else you can muster to move forward, one day at a time, doing your best to take care of your personal and professional lives.

You may find that demands on your time and attention are coming from all directions, even more so than usual. As you seek out information that is valuable and helpful, it is not uncommon to become overwhelmed—leading to a situation where you find that you are consuming too much information that is useless, distracting, and distressing.

What are your sources of trusted information? Where are the experts in your network? What organizations have you determined in the past to be useful, fact-based, and aligned with the way you process information? Figure out which sources work for you, tune into those sources, and do your best to drown out all the rest of the noise.

Trust is key. If you are a leader of anything—self, family, team, company, community—there are people who are counting on you to provide clear direction and accurate updates. To do that, and to maintain sanity, think critically about how much information you need to consume, and from what sources.

During challenging times, take a moment to consider: who or what do you trust? Focus on those people and those things.

Finally, be uncompromising

Don't compromise your commitment to do what you need to do so that you remain healthy, whole, sane, and fully capable of acting in the manner expected of you as a leader.

An empty tank helps no one. During times of trouble, you will have many people depending on you. You will be asked for information you may not have, and you will be asked to provide certainty where there are only unanswered questions. To stand in your power during difficult times, you need to replenish your power regularly. Do the things that you need to do—eat well, exercise, make time for silent reflection. If you have a spiritual practice, don't neglect it. If you have rituals and routines that energize you, fiercely protect them. Even in situations where you are required to be present and produce around the clock, don't fool yourself into thinking you can be the leader that you need to be without taking the time to do what it takes to keep from running on fumes.

In summary: in times of crisis, ask yourself, "Who do I want to BE in the midst of this challenge?" Practice being that person.

When there are no clear answers to critical questions, the act of drawing from your core sense of who you are, what you believe, and what your values are can be grounding. History has shown us that every crisis, at some point, passes. Think about how you want to be perceived after the ordeal is over. Write the story that will be told on the other side of the test. Do you appear in that story as someone who was hot-headed, erratic, reckless, destructively pessimistic, or unable to function in the midst of ambiguity? Or, as someone who was level-headed, decisive, empathetic, pragmatically optimistic, and effective? In trying times, things move fast, but in every decision that needs to be made, you have a choice: who do you want to be? Use the information you have gathered from your learning practice, lean into your core, and move in alignment with the answer to that question.

A lifelong learner who loves laughter, words, big ideas, and serving her community, **Ekpedeme "Pamay" M. Bassey** is chief learning officer for The Kraft Heinz Company and chief experience officer of The My 52 Weeks of Worship Project, through which she facilitates courageous conversations about cultural and interfaith diversity and understanding.

Pamay's TEDx talk, Navigating Sacred Spaces, is based on her project work and her book: *My 52 Weeks of Worship: Lessons from a Global, Spiritual, Interfaith Journey.* She is a graduate of Stanford, Northwestern and the Second City Conservatory program in Chicago.

BREAKING AND REBUILDING

Ayse Birsel

Time of crisis is when you deconstruct and reconstruct.

Leadership in crisis is a moment of forced deconstruction. Whether you like it or not, the crisis now is forcing you to deconstruct everything you know. You can either let it happen on its own or you can do a controlled collapse and rebuild.

Mark Thompson, America's No. 1 executive coach for growth companies, calls this emerging leadership behavior "burning down the house," inspired by Virgin founder Sir Richard Branson's account of rebuilding his house after it burned to the ground.

The times call for transformation, but none of us can afford to let it just happen. Rather, here's how we can do it intentionally.

Great American designer Charles Eames saw constraints as opportunities. When he was creating the winning entry for the Museum of Modern Art's 1941 design competition, he did more than 450 permutations of potential ideas, until he hit on the winning one. This kind of logical yet creative thinking is what's called for at times of crisis.

"Design depends largely on constraints." Eames said.

The method I want to share with you is **Deconstruction:Reconstruction™**. It is the proprietary process we use to help leading companies generate disruptive ideas that use what they know to arrive at fundamentally different outcomes.

Step 1 is to map out what your business is made up of—its main functions, services, strengths. This is Deconstruction.

Step 2 is to view these parts in the context of the transformation or crisis you're in. This is forming a POV.

Step 3 is putting the parts back together in new ways and generating as many permutations as possible. This is Reconstruction.

Following this process, you and your team can take the whole apart, look at the parts, decide what's essential and you need to keep, what's essential but needs to be transformed, and what needs to be thrown out. You can then put them back together in different ways and create multiple permutations. And every time you change an element, you will be changing your business model.

Let's look at the restaurant business in this time of crisis and we can see this collapse and rebuilding happening in front of our eyes.

RESTAURANT BUSINESS

EXPERTS IN FOOD	GATHERING SPACE	DINING EXPERIENCE	LOCAL BUSINESS	EXPERTS IN SANITATION
FOOD PANTRY	CLEANING SUPPLIES	LOYAL CUSTOMERS	TRUSTED BRAND	MAKING FOOD

What are the basic parts of a restaurant business? I listed them above. They're experts in food, they're local gathering places, Grade A certified in food sanitation, they have a food pantry, etc.

Now let's look at the changes. What are the specific internal or external conditions you need to respond to? Below are the specific conditions under COVID-19. Our POV is filtered through these conditions.

Let's go back and relook at the Deconstruction map. The current circumstances are forcing restaurants to take some of their key building blocks out of the equation, like being a gathering space and creating dining experiences.

What you need to do next is look at the other building blocks to see if you can combine them in new ways to keep your business afloat. You start making permutations, very much like a mathematical equation.

Above is one permutation mapped out. Many restaurants, including Los Angeles-based Dog Haus and Frisch's Big Boy, in Kentucky, Ohio, and Indiana, are now becoming neighborhood corner stores, selling takeout food, food ingredients, and cleaning supplies. They're reinventing themselves by recombining existing parts in new ways.

Another model is premium restaurants offering takeout, and in the case of the high-end Seattle restaurant, Canlis, becoming a drive-through. See it mapped out as an equation below.

You're getting the hang of it. To generate more permutations, look at other industry transformations for inspiration, like the one below that takes its cues from universities moving their courses online. Below is an online teaching model cross-fertilized with the restaurant model.

PERMUTATION #3 : ONLINE COURSES

EXPERTS   TRUSTED   LOYAL   FILMING OF   GLOBAL
IN FOOD   BRAND   CUSTOMERS   MAKING   REACH
                                           FOOD

You can take a restaurant's expertise in making food and add filming to it to generate online food-making courses. Your loyal customers can act as your ambassadors to generate awareness on social media to scale your reach from local to global.

What if you offered working parents who are now sheltering at home with their children a subscription model for affordable family meals?

You can continue and generate other permutations of your own.

Next, let's look at what British brand Dyson is doing. This is another example of how a successful, but not "essential," business can deconstruct its expertise and reconstruct it to respond to an essential need—ventilators.

The strength of the Dyson brand is managing air. All their products, from vacuums to blow dryers to hand dryers, deal with moving air. Dyson in this moment of crisis is a natural fit for making ventilators. Even so, to be able to do this in a timely fashion, they need to break their current business model and rejigger a new one. Below is my unedited Deconstruction:Reconstruction map of Dyson that helped me think this transformation through.

What Dyson did was take their expertise in air and partner with another company with expertise in health care, The Technology Partners. Next, they threw out their signature, complex, and recognizable injected molded plastic parts with long lead times in favor of parts made out of flat stock and bent metal processes that lend themselves to fast manufacturing.

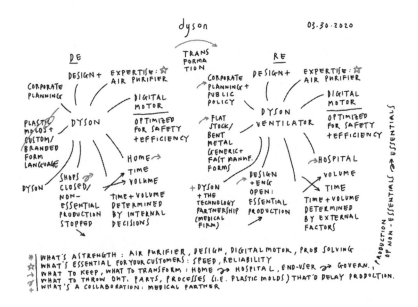

Both businesses responded in real time by breaking their businesses and rebuilding them. They kept what's essential, transformed what's transformable, and deleted what wasn't essential or sustainable.

Here are simple guidelines if you'd like to experiment with deconstructing and reconstructing your business in a controlled manner.

Deconstruct your business

Use these four prompts to break your business into its parts:

- What's your core business?
- What are the strengths of your brand?
- What was essential to your business and is it still?
- What was essential to your customers and is it still?

Form a POV

List the changes caused by the crisis at hand. Today, our context is COVID-19 at its peak. Tomorrow it will be post-COVID conditions. You can use these two prompts to consider both:

- What can you keep but need to transform, in the new context?
- What do you need to throw out, in this new context?

Reconstruct your business

Put back the parts back together in new ways to generate as many permutations as possible.

- What are short-term transformations?
- What are long-term transformations?
- What are short-term transformations with long-term benefits?
- What are new collaborations and partnerships?

Do this logically and systematically, mathematically. Include even seemingly bad ideas as some of the best ideas come from worst places. For more on this, check out my *Harvard Business Review* article, "To Come Up with a Good Idea, Start by Imagining the Worst Idea Possible."[1]

You can add your own to any of the above prompts, some of which will emerge as you're mapping things out.

Break and remake your business using this controlled model to transform it from a nonessential to an essential business in times of crisis.

Ayse Birsel is one of *Fast Company*'s Most Creative People 2017 and is on the Thinkers50 Radar List of the thirty management thinkers

---

1. https://hbr.org/2017/08/to-come-up-with-a-good-idea-start-by -imagining-the-worst-idea-possible

most likely to shape the future of organizations. She is the author of *Design the Life You Love.* Recognized as #1 Coach in Life Design by Marshall Goldsmith Leading Coaches, she gives lectures on Design the Life + Work You Love to corporations, Ayse is the co-founder of Birsel + Seck, the award-winning design and innovation studio, and consults to Amazon, Colgate-Palmolive, Herman Miller, GE, IKEA, The Scan Foundation, Staples, and Toyota, among others. Her design process, Deconstruction:Reconstruction™, is the red thread across all her work. Her work can be found in the permanent collection of the Museum of Modern Art (MoMA).

A THOUSAND PIVOT POINTS: RHIZOMIC LEADERSHIP AND THE CALL TO RISE

Jenny Blake

A time of crisis is a call to evolve. If we were asleep or on autopilot, perhaps even coasting on successes and flush markets, the urgency of a global pandemic shakes us awake and offers just one choice: step into the new reality or get left behind. This is a call to root down into our strengths and then rise—as leaders, as team members, and as organizations—but expect it to be nonlinear, messy, and rhizomic.

In botany, a rhizome is an underground stem that grows continuously and horizontally, forming lateral shoots and adventitious roots that grow upward or outward. Possibilities occur at every nodal intersection, like the networked maps of plane routes at the back of airline magazines. In their book *A Thousand Plateaus* (1980), philosophers Gilles Deleuze and Félix Guattari adapted the term to describe nonhierarchical, ever-expanding works-in-progress. Always forming, changing, and adapting, there is no *there* there. "A rhizome has no beginning or end; it is always in the middle, between things, interbeing, intermezzo," the authors write. The key advantage of rhizomic systems

23

is the electricity at these crossing points, the profusion of opportunity at countless nonhierarchical intersections. Advantage can erupt from anywhere two tendrils cross. The rhizome is the essence of a democratic system, or organization; wisdom can be found everywhere, in all nodes of collaboration and creativity.

During times of crisis and massive upheaval, we face not *a thousand plateaus* but *a thousand pivot points*. The choice is to pivot or get pivoted. Sometimes both happen: we get pivoted, and we choose how to respond and adapt, creating a new order from chaos as we strengthen ourselves as organizations, teams, and individuals.

When writing my second book, *Pivot: The Only Move That Matters Is Your Next One* (Portfolio/Penguin Random House, 2016), I developed the mantra "If change is the only constant, let's get better at it." I couldn't have imagined the massive upheaval the COVID-19 pandemic would incite around the world, when we would all be asked to navigate unprecedented change and uncertainty. When shelter-at-home practices swept across cities and nations, it was as if the pandemic hit a "pause" button on the planet.

Our new narrative continues writing itself. We are all starring in a play that has no third act in sight. As Deleuze and Guattari write, "The rhizome presents history and culture as a map, a wide array of attractions with no specific origin, no beginning—no end—always in the middle between things, ceaselessly establishing connections between a sequence of chains, organizations, and power—in art, science, politics, and social struggle."

How is anyone to navigate a constructive path in such a tumultuous environment? Even among traditional leaders, it is difficult to discern who among them is best equipped to navigate our rhizomic tangle of unceasing change.

High net worth individuals have accumulated significant financial resources; they certainly have an advantage when it comes to extending and leveraging their financial Pivot runway. But those who shine most during crises are *high net growth*, independent of financial worth. They know money is important, but it is not everything. They do not just ask, "What am I *earning?*" but "What am I *learning?* How am I growing? How am I serving, and making an impact?" Leaders asking these questions are *impacters.*

Like the rhizome, impacter leaders are called during crises to imagine new nodes of intersection and innovation to help us all grow (and simply survive). This process unfolds in a nonlinear manner if we let ourselves develop in crisis and not be sidelined by it. We extend roots toward our strengths and what's working—as individuals and organizations; then with this clarity we rise toward a higher vision. In rhizomic reality there are no dead ends; all paths are continuous, with no beginning and no end, and the sparks occur at random intersection points. This is where new solutions can emerge. Change is constant, but evolution is rare.

Expect this to be messy. Trust that when the tide recedes there will trash *and* treasure to sort. Prepare for the emotional roller-coaster and exhaustion that follows. At the same time, periods of crisis equip us with unique tools for sorting, exploring, and weighing options: clearer intuition, deeper introspection, superpowers of analysis, and neurochemicals and hormones not readily in use when the wind is at our backs.

I developed a four-stage framework, the Pivot Method, to help individuals and organizations map what's next. When a basketball player stops dribbling, one foot stays *planted* (their foundation) while their *pivot* foot steadies them as they scan for passing options. Or consider plotting your desired destination in Google Maps: only when you know where you're starting, and your general destination, does it make sense to consider timing, routes, modes of transport, and potential obstacles (such as traffic, accidents, or road closures). The mistake most pivoters (and leaders) make is jumping to problem solving too soon, with no grounding in what's already working best and envisioning what success looks like.

Reflect on these four Pivot stages for your organization (and ask your team members to do the same): for the entire company, for specific mission-critical projects, and as individuals.

1. Plant

What's working? What are your biggest strengths? What makes you unique? What does success look like? (During times of crisis, I recommend asking the last question at whatever interval makes most sense: during daily pivots you might focus on one week, or expand to one month, three months, six months, or a year—too far beyond that and most plans become irrelevant.)

2. Scan

Examine people, skills, and projects related to your strengths and vision. Who is thriving? Who can you talk to? Who do you admire? Who has already been helpful to you (or served as a client or mentor) in the past? How must you grow to meet your vision for success? Based on your strengths, how can you serve?

3. Pilot

What small experiments can you run as a team or organization, both short term and long term? Which pilots are relatively safe and conservative, and which ones are bigger bets? What pilots reflect asymmetric bets, where the upside greatly outweighs any potential downside? What smaller career pilots or stretch projects can individuals run to test the waters of a new related direction, even within their current role?

4. Launch

What one next step would make the biggest impact? What one small step can you take today or this week? What does a bigger launch look like for pilots that develop momentum and traction?

Like the rhizome, the Pivot Method is a cycle, not a one-and-done linear process. You can apply this to your team dynamics, the broader organization's strategy, and as a coaching framework for one-to-one conversations. During times of upheaval, your team is already more stretched and stressed than usual. Your employees, colleagues, friends, and family need you more than ever during a crisis. There is no need to have all the answers. Answers emerge while exploring. In the rhizome, stasis is death. Now is the time to have conversations with team members about change, anxiety, uncertainty, and the daily pivots large and small that you are navigating together. Facilitate these conversations by doubling down on what *is* working. Narrow your success cone of vision to one week or one month from now, as businesses and the surrounding milieu continues to shift rapidly from one day to the next. Sometimes it feels like one month passes each week. There is no way around it, only through; each day brings a new mental, emotional, or work project roller-coaster. If we can acknowledge this—and reframe our instinctive fears into opportunities for growth, innovation, and imagination—we can emerge stronger, and unquestionably smarter. We will be marked, but not scarred by the crisis.

If your team is feeling particularly frazzled or frozen from the daily snow globe shake-up of work and life shifts, try asking (or having them journal) the following reflection prompts:

- How are you doing?
- How have you already adapted?
- How are you growing during this time? How are you being called to evolve?
- How can you serve based on your strengths?
- Reverse engineer past pivots: How have you successfully navigated change in the past? What was the pivot that brought you to this organization? What pivots have you already made within your role or within the company?

Ultimately, the Pivot Method is about *listening* more than talking; *exploring* more than solving; and *experimenting* more than having all the answers—and that goes for leaders too—especially during times like these, when it's tempting to comfort others by jumping straight to problem solving and providing answers.

Those answers may take their time to unfold, pulling us significantly past our comfort zones. Nature doesn't rush a tree. The rhizomic roots within all of us are expanding, far below the surface. As a planet we are similarly more networked and interconnected than ever. There is superconscious intelligence available if we can get quiet enough to listen. As Rainer Maria Rilke writes in *Letters to a Young Poet*: "We have changed, as a house that a guest has entered changes. We can't say who has come, perhaps we will never know, but many signs indicate that the future enters us in this way in order to be transformed in us, long before it happens."

A parting thought from Greek philosopher Heraclitus: "No man ever steps in the same river twice, for it's not the same river, and he's not the same man." As rhizomic leaders, we expand, we rise, and we flow. Every day is an opportunity to grow stronger and help others do the same, so long as we drop our expectations about neat predictable paths along the way.

Jenny Blake, author of *Pivot: The Only Move That Matters is Your Next One* and *Pivot* podcast host, works with innovative organizations on navigating change and helping individuals map what's next. Her motto? If change is the only constant, let's get better at it.

VALIDATION

Peter Bregman

"I'm feeling deeply unsettled," my client we'll call Keller, the CEO of an investment firm, said to me.

"Of course," I *could* reply, "we're in unsettling times! Especially for you, a CEO whose organization is disrupted. You're worried about cash and operational continuity. And you're in the investment community. How can you not be unsettled in the face of such dramatic and unpredictable market swings? I totally get it."

That would have been the most obvious next thing for me to say. It would reflect my empathy, my understanding, my connection, my own knowledge and expertise. We'd both feel good about the exchange.

But it would have been a mistake.

A mistake because, especially in this very new, unique moment, there's a response that's even more powerful when someone expresses their vulnerability. A response that's important and necessary *before* empathy.

Curiosity.

Because the truth is, I don't know what's going on for Keller. In fact, *Keller* hardly knows what's going on for Keller. We're on new ground here.

And while everything I could have said *could* have been true, I don't really know what *is* true. Which means that before *demonstrating* my understanding, I have to *develop* it. I need to ask questions and be open and listen and learn.

Which takes humility. Humility is *not* knowing. And that, eventually and almost always, leads to empathy, which leads to compassion. A deeper, more real, empathy and a more meaningful compassion.

So when Keller told me he was feeling deeply unsettled, I asked him to tell me more. I'm glad I did.

See, Keller didn't talk to me about his role as CEO, his operational challenges, or his investments. He's a solid leader, and like so many other solid leaders I know, he's sure-footed and capable in times of crisis.

No, Keller wasn't struggling as a *leader*. He was struggling as a *human being*.

Keller talked about feeling scared and lonely and sad and a little lost. He's feeling the weight of these times, of the uncertainty in human life. He's feeling the challenges of his family and the psychological shift of being alone in his house vs. in an office.

One effect of social distancing and working from home is that we are left, much more than usual, with ourselves. That can lead to some loss of our sense of self. Who are we when we are no longer reflected in the faces of the people around us? Do we even know who we are, without all the external recognition?

External recognition helps us define ourselves. People in the office say we look good. We receive praise for a job well done. Someone does something that disturbs or even enrages us. All those things tell us who we are.

What's left when we can no longer rely on that feedback, on the external mirrors and projections other people shine on us?

What's left is ourselves. At home, working through a screen, we're left with ourselves.

We're just people—in underwear and pajamas—alone or maybe with children in rooms nearby watching screens or screaming or playing spike ball. No fancy clothes and cars to project an image. No praise or even rejection. No feedback at all to define us.

And that can leave us feeling lost. Or, as Keller put it, unsettled.

Maybe you're feeling a little of that?

I know I am. In a day, I feel everything, often inexplicably. Joy and sadness. Thrill and anger. Frustration and ease. And, of course, fear. But also, of course, excitement and connection.

To feel it all requires courage. Emotional courage.

Which is why, as important and difficult as it is to stay curious about others, there's something equally important—and far more difficult—to do:

Stay curious about ourselves.

That is what is required of us now, in this new moment. A moment that is not simple, clear, or expected. Being curious about ourselves is how we begin to know—really know—who we are. That can be scary. But also, possibly, exciting and freeing.

The hardest part? Slowing down enough to actually feel. Especially when everyone else is moving faster than ever. Do you have the courage to slow down?

Because slowing down will, by its very nature, bring up feelings. And that can feel depressing.

And so we move. Over the past few weeks, I have often felt lost, surrounded by people scrambling to move. They are making plans, pivoting their businesses, voicing opinions, networking, setting direction, filling their schedules with Zoom calls.

I'm on some of those Zoom calls and when, after listening to how everyone else is pivoting, people ask me how I'm pivoting, my answer is, "I don't know."

I don't know what to do. I am not driven to act. And that scares me. What if I'm left behind? And then it occurs to me that that is one of the reasons I act. And it is the wrong reason to act. So I don't act. And when I don't act, all I'm left with is me.

And then it occurs to me that, maybe, painfully, this is part of what this moment is about: I am learning about myself.

It is, I believe, deeply important to honor our *not knowing*. And to be curious about ourselves in the process.

There is a way in which this pandemic may be calling us to slow down and listen. We are often so certain—about everything—that we don't slow down enough to listen. What if we resist the urge to act—to just do something—and, instead, just be present. To ourselves first. Discover what's there. And then, when we're on solid ground, act out of that place.

Who are you?

If you survive this pandemic, answering that question might be the most important thing that comes out of it for you. The slowing down, the not knowing, the humility—that, to me, is turning out to be what this moment is about.

Because here's the truth: We know very little. Almost nothing. Maybe nothing.

We don't know when this will end. Or how. And we don't know what it will look like as it takes its course. We don't know if we—or people we love—will get sick. And if we get sick, we don't know if we will survive. I have already lost people I never expected to lose—lovely, sweet, generous people.

We don't know what the market will do today or tomorrow or next week or next year. We don't know what will happen to our economy or to our neighborhoods.

We just don't know. We can pretend to know. We can listen to pundits and try to learn and seek to know. But we just don't know. We can't.

And that, perhaps, can be a gift of this moment. The recognition that we don't know and the curiosity to see, to listen, to notice. First, to be curious about others, because that's easier.

And then to be curious about ourselves. To slow down and notice what you're feeling. And when you notice, don't push it away or be hard on yourself or act your way into an escapist frenzy. Instead, do what you would do for others—listen and empathize. And from that place of empathy, feel compassion. For yourself.

So, I ask you, in this moment, can you stop everything for a beat, take a breath, and be curious?

What are you feeling?

Recognized as the #1 executive coach in the world by *Leading Global Coaches*, **Peter Bregman** coaches CEOs and senior leaders in many of the world's premier organizations. He is the award-winning, best selling author and contributor of sixteen books, including, most recently, *Leading with Emotional Courage.*

THE POWER OF 'I DON'T KNOW'

David Burkus

In times of crisis, we chase certainty. When the entire world seems like it's changing around us, and there is no way we can change it back to the way it was, our natural tendency is to latch on to anything that looks like it won't change any more. In a tumultuous sea, we look for any signs of land. As a result, we often find ourselves following any leader who offers the illusion of certainty—even if it's only an illusion.

Even under normal circumstances, it's easy to mistake confidence and the appearance of certainty for competence. Somewhere along the way, we decided that decisiveness was a mark of a good leader. And then we started promoting the most confident deciders . . . even if their decisions were terrible. We vote for the ones who reassure us with their confidence, and then watch as they blame unforeseen circumstances for their failure (despite those circumstances often being quite foreseen).

The logical end to all this is that now we struggle with leaders in all domains confidently asserting their thoughts on a certain issue or confidently presenting the solution to a problem they've just learned about. We hear that confidence in their voice, and it can become all too easy to assume it means they're presenting a well-thought-out plan. They look so certain, and so we follow hoping we can catch some of that precious certainty.

And in a crisis, we can end up following that certain-looking but incompetent leader right off a cliff.

The truth is, there is little correlation between confidence and competence. In fact, it can often go the opposite way. More than twenty years ago, psychologists David Dunning and Justin Kruger demonstrated that when people knew very little about a topic or situation, they were very likely to overassess their knowledge and ability. The less they knew, the more confident they were in their expertise. The more they learned, the more they realized how much there was to learn and the humbler they became about their own competence. And most important, the humbler they became, the more they sought out more information to increase their expertise and make a better decision.

A similar pattern occurs with teams and leaders. In a study led by psychologist Amy Brunell, leaderless teams often sought out the same two qualities in electing the team's leader: narcissism and overconfidence. When no one knew what to do or even who to look to, they most often started looking to the people whose primary "leadership" quality was a desire for others to look at them. They wanted attention, and had the overconfidence needed to get that attention. But overconfidence in leadership often means ignoring the facts that don't fit our existing mental model, and rarely seeking to alleviate that ignorance.

Ignorance isn't bliss; it's confidence. And confident ignorance can lead to disaster.

For leaders, a powerful antidote is simply acknowledging that you don't know. When you're asked a question that you don't know the answer to, just say "I don't know" and then commit to finding the answer. When you are asked for your advice on a situation, you can just say, "I don't know. Let me think more and get back to you." Beyond giving you the opportunity to find the right answer, "I don't know" communicates your own intellectual curiosity and your intellectual humility.

Yes, you have to be committed to finding out. And yes, you should probably share with people when you do know. But asserting with a pigheaded certainty that you already know is far more damaging than admitting "I don't know" and then taking the time for you and your team to find out.

The power of "I don't know" can even be extended to situations where followers seem to truly need some certainty. Making a decision or announcing a plan of action, based on limited information—even when it's done not from overconfidence but from a desire to provide much-needed certainty—can backfire in the same way that overconfident leaders wrongly assert their ignorance. Instead of making the decision in the moment and providing an illusion of certainty, consider announcing the date by which a decision will be made. It doesn't provide the same feeling of certainty as a firm decision—but it acknowledges the truth: that a firm decision can't be made today and it would be more harmful in the long run to make one.

The power of "I don't know" even has a spillover effect of sending a message to your people that it's okay not to have all the answers. It creates a form of psychological safety that people around you don't have to hide their doubts. And when people share their doubts and questions, we all benefit by examining the topic or issue more to resolve those questions.

While confidence and certainty are what most followers think they want in a crisis, what they really want is a competent leader who can minimize the damage and steer them safely through the storm. Competent leaders are almost always humble leaders: their humility allows them to keep seeking out more information and make the best decision when the time is right for a decision.

If you want a culture where finding the right answer is valued more than faking the right answer—if you want a culture of actual competence and not just confident ignorance—then get used to saying "I don't know" more and encouraging those around you to do the same.

David Burkus is a best-selling author, a sought-after speaker, and business school professor. He's the author of four books, including his newest, *Pick a Fight*, and a regular contributor to *Harvard Business Review*. He has delivered keynotes to Fortune 500 companies and his TED talk has been viewed over two million times.

A MESSAGE FROM THE QUEEN

James M. Citrin

On April 5, 2020, Queen Elizabeth, sequestered in Windsor Castle, addressed her nation in a rare televised speech.

"I am speaking to you at what I know is an increasingly challenging time," the queen said with her trademark steady yet compassionate voice. "A disruption that has brought grief to some, financial difficulties to many, and enormous changes to the daily lives of us all." With the virus having infected over 40,000 people in Britain as of that moment, including her seventy-one-year-old son, Prince Charles, she captivated the British people and millions around the world with a speech that hearkened back to the gravest days of World War II.

This was only the fourth televised address in her sixty-eight-year reign, apart from her annual televised Christmas speeches, which began in 1957. She delivered a powerful leadership moment, coinciding with the day that Prime Minister Boris Johnson, infected with the coronavirus, checked into the hospital and soon thereafter into intensive care. As a result, the audience listened intently to the queen's urging to bring extra resolve to the hardships to come and a dedication to fighting the crisis.

Talking in terms both deeply personal and historic, the queen recalled the sacrifices families made during World War II, when parents were forced to send their children out of London to protect them from the Luftwaffe bombings. She acknowledged the financial pain and hardships that Britons have been enduring and thanked the National Health Service for their dedication. And she urged a population that takes pride in its "Keep Calm and Carry On" attitude to maintain the discipline to stay home and safely socially distant.

"Today, once again, many will feel a painful sense of separation from their loved ones," she said. "But now, as then, we know, deep down, that it is the right thing to do." And she concluded with the uplifting message, "We will meet again," which was especially poignant for the beloved ninety-four-year-old queen.

Helped by the Royal Family's social media-savvy team, she also capitalized on the latest tools to amplify her message. Just as her original televised Christmas speech was the first to be broadcast live sixty-three years ago, her address generated over three million likes on Instagram within sixteen hours of the broadcast (@theroyalfamily has 7.7 million Instagram followers).

The queen's speech, which one commentator said "struck not a single false note," is an example of a key principle of leadership in a time of crisis: to confront a challenge realistically, give voice to how people are feeling, put it in a proper context, and provide clear communications about what it means for you and me.

Leadership by example

Whether as a parent, an entry-level manager, or a CEO, an effective leader wants to model the behavior and attitudes they want to instill. But in a time of crisis, leadership by example is more important and impactful than ever. People rally around their leaders in times of crisis. That's why approval ratings of political leaders usually soar in a crisis. Across companies and organizations, employees and other stakeholders look to their leaders for signs of hope and direction. And as a leader, you have no better way to influence the actions and mindsets of others than to embody the behaviors and attitudes you'd like to propagate.

Barry Sternlicht, a legend of the global hospitality and real estate industry as founder of Starwood Capital, Starwood Hotels & Resorts, and SH Hotels & Resorts, did just this at the height of the COVID-19 crisis. He issued a heartfelt appeal to the loyal guests and visitors of his hotels, asking for financial support for furloughed employees. "As we navigate these previously unnavigated roads," he wrote in a personal email to all guests who had visited one of the hotels, "it's important to remember that we must be able to lean on one another during these tough times." Then he put his employees first. "To say that our award-winning teams are at the heart of our success is an understatement. Unfortunately, like the millions of hospitality professionals across the world, so many of our team are hurting financially because of suspended services and closures required to comply with health guidelines."

To address this, he created Starwood Cares Employee Relief Fund; he and the company's leadership team donated a significant amount to seed the fund. But beyond doing that, Sternlicht pledged this: "Because you, our guests and loyal fans, are what drive us all to deliver exceptional experiences, I want to encourage you to join us in our support." And he personally pledged to match the contributions of others from outside the company.

Sternlicht is not the only corporate leader who has pledged financial support to help respond to the pandemic. Others have done so and often in staggering amounts. Jack Dorsey, founder and CEO of both Square and Twitter, announced plans to donate $1 billion, nearly one-third of his net worth, to coronavirus relief programs. Jeff Bezos, Michael Dell, and Bill Gates have each pledged $100 million to vaccine development efforts and food banks, as have many others from Silicon Valley and Wall Street.

There is a difference with Sternlicht's efforts, however. While some of the other leaders were leading by example at a macro level, donating massive resources to find a cure for the dreaded virus, for example, Sternlicht's actions were designed to attack the problems at a more micro level. He demonstrated to his employees that he cared about them and then turned that care into action, at an architectural level, by designing and launching the fund, and at a personal level by giving a meaningful amount of money. In addition, he recognized that the guests and visitors who have had joyous experiences at the hotels would be motivated to follow Sternlicht 's example and show their support.

In so doing, Sternlicht was also able to create more intimate customer bonds. After all, if you can't go to one of the hotels or resorts during the crisis, at least you can still feel a connection to the brand and the satisfaction of making a financial contribution, all beautifully tech-enabled, to make it as simple as a few taps on your smartphone.

Other dimensions of leadership in a time of crisis

Other important ways exist to lead in a time of crisis. Many are familiar with the notion to "never let a good crisis go to waste." That is, to use the crisis as a catalyst to make the bold moves that may have been impossible in more robust times. A proverbial burning platform arising from external events may give leaders the fortitude and air cover to take difficult and bold decisions. In fact, when reviewing the winners coming out of the financial crisis of 2008,[1] found that the companies that mastered the delicate balance between cutting costs in order *to survive today* and investing *to grow tomorrow* did the best after the recession. More specifically, the companies that executed a particular combination of reducing costs selectively—to focus on operational efficiency rather than across-the-board cuts—while simultaneously investing boldly in the future—by spending on marketing, R&D, and new assets—had the highest probability of outpacing their peers coming out of the recession. Today's best leaders, managing through the current pandemic and economic fallout, will also strive to find the right blend of defensive and offensive moves.

On a related note, the most effective leaders during times of crisis are spurring innovation. As countless people around the world have now personally experienced, many companies, schools, and families have adapted long-held practices by operating remotely, keeping their activities running, making smart decisions, learning, and building camaraderie through Zoom. Some companies have also turned their design and manufacturing expertise from hairdryers or automobiles to making ventilators, or from fashion and apparel to making face masks.

---

1. *Roaring Out of Recession*, Ranjay Gulati, Nitin Nohria and Franz Wohlgezogen, March 2010, https://hbr.org/2010/03/roaring-out-of-recession

The old trope that necessity is the mother of invention has never been more true than today.

Conclusion

Leadership in a time of crisis is difficult. As a leader, you are constantly under pressure and will have little downtime. You surely don't know for yourself how bad things are going to get and how long the crisis is going to endure. And you don't have a crystal ball to tell you whether your actions are going work and enable you to thrive . . . or even survive.

All the same, a crisis creates a moment in time when people are receptive and more likely to embrace your leadership. They *want* you to step up and fill the void. You have their permission to be bold and courageous, especially if you acknowledge their pain and fears in a way that is genuine, authentic, and caring.

If you do, you can inspire others and lead them to feel connected, purposeful, and motivated to do what is necessary for the greater good. Leading by example, communicating in clear and grounded, yet appropriately hopeful ways, and making the smart decisions that will maximize the probability of setting you up for success on the other side, will allow you to look back with the satisfaction of knowing that you did your job as a leader.

James M. Citrin is a best-selling author of seven books on leadership, including *You're in Charge, Now What?* and *The Five Patterns of Extraordinary Careers*. He is a senior partner at executive search and leadership advisory firm Spencer Stuart, where he leads the firm's CEO practice.

COMMUNICATIONS CHANGE IN A CRISIS

Erica Dhawan

History tells us that each decade will host its own crisis. It's not a matter of *what if*, but *when*. As business leaders, we have a responsibility to use each experience to prepare for the next. So what lessons can we take from the coronavirus pandemic?

When company personnel are forced to work remotely during a crisis, gaps in organizational trust become glaringly obvious. Suddenly, leaders need to give up some of the power they've been hoarding and choose instead to empower their teams to take charge of their own work. Teammates need to reassess their information flow and can no longer carry on politics as usual. Chronic cancellations are no longer acceptable, and neither is passive-aggressive or coded language. In short, we are forced to innovate and rapidly evolve. The organizations that haven't built the operating system to work remotely are suffering. COVID-19 was, to them, a surprise.

Face-to-face communications are gone, and with them, the tonality and body language of our words—making communications (especially the intrinsically hard ones) difficult. Teams that haven't taken the time to focus on alignment no longer have face-to-face brainstorming time to get back on the same page and struggle with a lack of practice in video meetings. And companies with low psychological safety are seeing remote workers pull away—speaking up less, allowing themselves to become distracted, and assuming the worst intentions in their coworkers.

Meanwhile, the world is watching. Consumers are looking to see how business leaders respond to hardship. Are you being empathetic with your workforce? Are you asking them to work in unsafe conditions? Which CEOs are dutifully forgoing their own salaries to keep their companies running? And which businesses will survive? Mark Cuban has said that how companies treat workers during the pandemic could define their brand "for decades."

How must leaders adapt in times of crisis? Organizations worldwide have begun taking the necessary steps to build trust and combat the challenges that come with being thrust into remote work unprepared. We have to plan better for meetings, create agendas, and generally think more critically about leading through communications in crises. Amy Edmondson, Novartis Professor of Leadership and Management at Harvard Business School, believes that, during these times, "mastering the design and management of teams will become an even more critical focus." She observed that extended work-from-home requirements will bring "a shift away from static organizational structures toward dynamic team forms," which work well only "under conditions of psychological safety, when leaders have made it crystal clear that every team member is welcome to speak up with ideas, concerns, and, yes, bad news."[1]

So, what do these dynamic team communications look like in times of crisis?

Here are three key lessons to lead through strong communications in any type of crisis:

1. Develop communication norms prepared for information sharing across all types of channels—before you need them

During COVID-19, one team leader told me: "Every morning we start with Zoom all-hands meetings. We ask: *What did you do yesterday?*

---

1. "How the Coronavirus Is Already Rewriting the Future of Business," Harvard Business School Working Knowledge, March 15, 2020, https://hbswk.hbs.edu/item/how-the-coronavirus-is-already-rewriting-the-future-of-business

Today? And do you have any blockers? We also do another at the end of the day: *What worked? What didn't? What did we try?* It's a great way to celebrate our successes, share challenges, and create boundaries." This kind of dialog enables teams to become more vocal about their needs and, in turn, learn to communicate more clearly and efficiently.

Working remotely makes us feel disconnected. A way to solve that is to become excessively available and transparent. One of my clients has decided to leave his chat open during the entirety of his work hours. He's made IM the primary contact point between team members as it is most similar to the office dynamic of being able to walk past someone's desk or pop into their office. This way, his team members are confident that they can reach him and one another easily, even if it's not necessarily task-related. In periods of crises, speed of response matters even more than substance in some cases.

On that note, decide early on which technologies you will use for work-related tasks and what the expected response times are for each during periods of crisis. It can seem more egregious to take forty-eight hours to answer an email when you know the other person is likely at their computer all day. For example, one executive said, "We created clear communications protocol that included everyone's contact information; which communication channels we'll use—email, IM, Slack, etc.; how employees are expected to respond to customers; and how and when teams will coordinate and meet."

Whichever norms you implement, make sure you stick with them while also checking in with your teams about the efficacy and ease of their communications. If something isn't working, adapt. That's the name of the game in most crisis situations.

2. Create spaces for celebration and social connections

Research has shown that the things people miss the most when transitioning to remote work are the social, relationship-building activities that happen when we walk by someone's desk and say hello, meet in the breakroom and discuss our latest Netflix binge, or notice that someone seems distracted and ask if they're okay. It's the watercooler interactions. At one recruiting firm, a team discussed how they used virtual happy hours. "I had a virtual happy hour with about sixty of my colleagues. We laughed, celebrated, connected—saw some very cute kids and also pets in the background. We've committed to keeping this tradition going even after we go back to work. What a morale booster!" Seeing each person dressed down and more vulnerable, showcasing our homes to one another and sharing our anxieties, we tear down the facades used to "fit in" at work and show off our true selves. Other examples include sending a daily email with a poem or positive video, sharing weekly recipe Slack channels, or hosting a daily "morning Zoom coffee break." Creating virtual spaces and rituals for celebrations and socializing can strengthen relationships and lay the foundation for swift collaboration.

3. Live in a learning mindset and be comfortable with vulnerability

Older executives have found a unique revelation in all this—they have to face their vulnerabilities with informality and technology. Digital natives (read: those who had cellphones growing up) are the key to helping less-technical people navigate these digital tools, so don't be afraid to ask "how do I get to the chat button on Zoom" or "I don't know how to toggle on Hangouts." And if you have those skills, offer patience with those who are fumbling and making mistakes. More importantly, encouraging both executives and junior staff to learn from one another and adapt together is fundamental to these times. One HR leader told me: "I've noticed that we have to be willing to be uncomfortable. I've seen executive by executive willing to turn on video on Zoom slowly until finally everyone is on video. It's a significant change from the past." She continued, "I've also had to remind junior staff to ensure their video background is professional when on customer videos. It's fine to be informal with teammates, but we have to dress up a bit with customers." In many ways, if we are thoughtful about this cross-generational knowledge sharing, we realize digital offices are the future of work.

Through intentional communications, many teams begin to trust one another—out of necessity, sure, but the connections are invaluable regardless. "While it feels weird and clunky at first, video calls do work," said one employee. Stephanie, CEO of a wealth management firm who had never worked remotely in her twenty-year career, said, "I do feel connected actually." Connection is more than possible. It's happening.

As crises come and go, we must prepare to lead through effective communications. The solution will not come from new technologies, instead by building a communication skill set that reflects the demands of our digitally driven age.

Erica Dhawan is an expert on twenty-first-century collaboration. She is the coauthor of the best-selling book *Get Big Things Done: The Power of Connectional Intelligence* and hosts the award-winning podcast *Masters of Leadership*.

YOUR LEADERSHIP INFLUENCE, INTERRUPTED

Connie Dieken

The massive scale and unpredictability of this pandemic is placing extraordinary demands on your leadership influence. Every expectation has been altered; every life, changed. No behavior shift on planet Earth has ever spread so quickly and unequivocally—in business and beyond.

The other side of this worldwide cataclysm is that it's handing you a once-in-a-lifetime opportunity to reveal and raise your leadership influence for good. Let's examine it from this angle—because when you're an influential leader, you shape positive change faster, more completely, and for the long term.

When you're influential, people trust your judgment, respect your opinions, and listen for your voice. They seek your input, even if they disagree with you, and give you the benefit of the doubt.

The world's best leaders are influential in all directions, with all stakeholders, from their boards of directors and leadership teams to investors, employees, customers, and their communities, even under the most challenging conditions.

So how do you become more influential?

First, influence yourself

I'm a social scientist whose research focuses on how leaders attempt to change minds. Our twenty-year research study revealed that most leaders are persuasive, but not influential. That surprises many leaders, because they assume that their roles as leaders grant them influence. What's the difference between persuasion and influence? Sustainability. Persuasion is short term. It's perfectly fine for quick fixes, but it's inefficient, exhausting, and ultimately ineffective. Persuaders have to reinvent the wheel with every conversation. The trap of persuasion is that you're susceptible to the next act of persuasion that comes along.

Influence, on the other hand, is sustainable. This is the elite stage of leadership where you unify, elevate, and shape the future. And this is the opportunity that you have right now—to join the elite corps of leaders who truly influence positive, lasting change.

You can't influence a world that no longer exists

Your leadership influence has been on thin ice for years, whether you realized it or not. That's because the internet *democratized* influence. The pandemic has now *shattered* that.

The digital age ushered in endless resources for your stakeholders, put a library in every pocket to fact-check you, shrunk your timelines, and flattened your org charts. The already-hard-to-convince people in your life—the narcissists, highly anxious, and passive-aggressives—became even harder to convince under digital conditions.

And now, the great *equalizer* has arrived. The pandemic didn't just spread a virus rapidly; it also sped up the inevitable shift from top-down influence to peer-to-peer persuasion. It's time for all leaders to accept that influence is a *meritocracy*, not an autocracy. You have to *earn* the right to influence your stakeholders, not merely persuade them to do things or, heaven forbid, manipulate them for one-sided gain.

Adopt the three-step 'Influence Cycle'

Our *Influence360°* team discovered that the world's most influential leaders change hearts and minds by cycling through three skills.

They've mastered all three and know how and when to tap into each one.

The good news is that you've already made a habit of using at least one of these skills. After all, you didn't make it this far as a leader without applying at least one.

The key is to make it a habit to cycle through *all three*, in sequential order.

So, what are the skills in the Influence Cycle? They are *Connect, Convey, Convince.*®

Here's how you can build these skills during this challenging time and beyond.

Step 1: Connect. The purpose of connecting is to create openness.

Connecting doesn't mean "reaching out." Most corporate COVID-19 messages flooding your in-box fail to connect. You've read one, you've read them all.

Now more than ever, every leader must level up their ability to connect. This is a golden opportunity, while business-as-usual safeguards are interrupted, to hit the reset button on your approach to openness. To do this, start your interactions by identifying and sharing *common ground.*

Pay close attention to what your stakeholders are wrestling with and connect the dots between their concerns and values and your own. Here are a few ideas:

- I advise many of the CEOs I coach to send brief video messages to their teams and request thirty-second videos in response, sharing their primary concern or asking a question. The leaders are always shocked at how many responses they get.
- Don't go long stretches without connecting. Your intention may be to wait for solid facts to emerge, but when people are anxious, a lack of interaction is interpreted as a lack of openness.
- The people you lead don't want scripted responses that your communications team drew up. *They crave your humanity.* If you

can't deliver your authentic self, don't bother communicating at all. You will be ignored.

Worse, you'll unleash the *rumor mill*.
Rumor is the most potent form of connection. Rumors appeal to our human need to bond, gain respect, and be in the loop. If people perceive that you aren't sharing the truth, they'll fill the void with peer-to-peer speculation, full of worst-case scenarios that can undermine you.
Most leaders choose to ignore the rumor mill, thinking they can stay above it. But that's a mistake. You must pursue and foresee the thoughts and concerns that fuel it, both internally and externally.

Step 2: Convey. The world craves clarity in a crisis of this magnitude. Initial reactions are purely emotional as our primal fight-or-flight responses kick in. You've seen this with the early responses to the pandemic as people started acting without thinking, hoarding food and essentials like toilet paper.

Challenging conditions require leaders who can simplify to amplify; leaders who transform ambiguity into concrete messages, who convey the right information, in the right amount, at the right time.

This doesn't mean dumbing things down. To the contrary, influential leaders understand that conveying information is the complex business of simplicity.

Most leaders think they're very good at conveying information. But truth be told, they're not. Many leaders make things sound even more complex than they are. And when you confuse, you lose.

Which gives you another golden opportunity to raise your influence. Do the heavy lifting by *streamlining* information before you convey it. Here are three ways to streamline:

1. Show before you tell

Vision is our dominant sense. Neurologists say we absorb messages *ten times faster* through our eyes than our ears. That's why you should choose a strong visual to anchor your messages.

It helps people organize, analyze, and integrate new knowledge quickly.

This explains why the best leaders share tools like Johns Hopkins's coronavirus map.[1] It conveys a simple yet sophisticated message that establishes big picture context. They use it to anchor their core messages and commentary.

2. Talk in triplets

Turns out, three is the most influential number. Your mind craves information in multiples of three, making the humble trilogy a shortcut to conveying powerful messages when people are feeling overwhelmed.

Three feels satisfying without being overwhelming, which is why it's so effective to structure your messages in three segments.

What specific triplets should you use in times of uncertainty? It depends upon what information will best serve your audience, but here's an example:

1. What you currently know about the situation.
2. What you don't know.
3. What you're doing to fill in those knowledge gaps.

3. Share stories

Stories help people process complex information quickly. They have a longer shelf life than mere facts because they bring information to life in a compelling narrative that people can share with others.

You need to tell only two types of stories in a crisis: success stories and cautionary tales. The best way to identify what type of story to tell is to start with the end in mind. Reverse engineer your story from the specific lesson that you want to illustrate.

Step 3: Convince. Convincing is the ability to unify and earn commitment. The dirty little secret of convincing is that you don't convince anyone of anything—they convince *themselves*.

---

1. https://coronavirus.jhu.edu/map.html

Regardless of our position or power, we each get to choose for ourselves whether we commit our hearts and minds to something or someone.

Our research shows that people are more likely to commit when they're at the height of emotion, during the initial rush. But *maintaining* that level of commitment and *keeping people unified* is the challenge. After the dust settles, people naturally start splintering, which leads to heightened resistance. Which brings us back to the importance of the *Influence Cycle*. It's a recurring sequence, not a one-and-done mission. The world's most influential leaders continually monitor and cycle through the skills of connecting, conveying, and convincing.

Influence is a choice

The collective actions we're taking to keep one another safe amid the disruption are heartening. We're witnessing countless acts of courage and sacrifice that we'll remember for the rest of our lives.

This pause also provides a once-in-a-lifetime opportunity for us to reflect and focus on what lies ahead, in the eventual reboot.

Let's use this interruption to strengthen our organizations, the people we serve—and our personal leadership influence—to emerge even better than before.

Connie Dieken is a social scientist whose research focuses on leadership influence. She advises C-suite executives at the world's leading brands on how to influence positive outcomes in all directions under challenging conditions. The founder and chairman of The Dieken Group, Dieken developed and launched Influence360°, a statistically validated research tool that measures influence patterns.

HOW CAPACITY BUILDING WILL HELP

Robert Glazer

We learn the most about leadership by observing leaders in times of crisis. Recently we've seen many examples of this as business and civic leaders respond to the unprecedented threat of COVID-19.

The leaders who are excelling during this time of adversity are taking accountability and focusing on helping others rather than assigning blame. They are resilient in the face of sleepless nights and long hours. They have a clear sense of purpose and communicate complex information with clarity and precision.

While some in leadership positions are struggling and operating from a place of fear, the most effective leaders are rising to the occasion and motivating their teams to follow their example. Many of these inspiring leaders have prepared themselves for this moment by building their capacity.

Capacity building is the method by which we seek, acquire, and develop the skills and abilities that help us to consistently perform at a higher level and develop our innate potential. It is an incremental process of intentional improvement in four areas: spiritual, intellectual, physical, and emotional capacity.

Capacity building isn't just about improving ourselves. When leaders build their capacity, they inspire the people they lead to do the same. When these leaders take charge in a crisis, they compel others to come together and support one another, even if it means sacrificing for the greater good.

Capacity building is crucial to crisis leadership as each of the four elements plays a vital role in thriving under adversity. Here's how:

Spiritual Capacity: Clarify what matters most

There are two types of leaders in a crisis, the Blamer and the Unifier. The Blamer constantly flails to address the various challenges they are faced with every day and is always looking to place blame when things go wrong. The Unifier has a clear purpose and strategy, communicates it well to others, and keeps the team focused and unified.

Spiritual capacity is about understanding who you are, what you want most, and what standards you want to live by each day. This is best defined as your purpose and core values. While these standards often apply to a long-term orientation, developing your spiritual capacity can help you clarify a short-term purpose that will keep you and your team focused and connected during a challenging time.

For example, as our company navigates the public health and economic challenges of COVID-19, I've clarified my short-term purpose: keep as many people employed as possible. It's what literally gets me out of bed each day and it's a unifying purpose our team has rallied around. I've been inspired to see our team members brainstorm a year's worth of innovations in just a few weeks to help our clients and one another.

When you're laser focused in a crisis, the people you lead will emulate that commitment and will raise their game as a result.

Intellectual Capacity: Lead by learning

Intellectual capacity is about how you improve your ability to think, learn, plan, and execute with discipline. If you've spent years improving your knowledge and discipline, you'll be able to get more done and make faster decisions in situations where quick action makes all the difference.

However, intellectual capacity isn't just about what you know; it's about recognizing what you *don't* know and leaning on experts to supplement your knowledge. Leaders who think they know every-thing will inevitably lead people in the wrong direction. This is espe-cially true in a complicated crisis such as COVID-19.

I'm seeing many CEOs turning to peer mentoring groups and mas-termind organizations to share what is working in responding to COVID-19 as well as what is not. Many of these CEOs are benefiting from the wisdom of those leaders whose businesses survived the 2008 recession—and they are applying those lessons quickly. The leaders who think they know it all will fall dangerously far behind over the course of this crisis.

Strong leaders reach out to experts and to those smarter than them-selves to educate themselves on what they need to know. For instance, if you run a restaurant, you need to learn how to quickly and effec-tively run a delivery service. If you're in retail, the focus right now should be learning how to build your online services. Committing to increasing your intellectual capacity will guide you and your team through complicated, high-pressure situations.

Physical Capacity: Withstand the grind

Physical capacity is your health, well-being, and physical performance. Building physical capacity isn't as simple as diet and exercise—it's also about prioritizing sleep and handling stress with resilience.

I'm not an advocate for working extraordinarily long hours as a reg-ular practice. But in wartime, the typical conventions around work aren't the same. To navigate through, many leaders are having to go above and beyond, including working nights and weekends.

At the same time, it's important to ensure that your body and mind are holding up so you can get the results you need. That includes know-ing how to make time to reset and rest, getting outside, taking planned breaks, napping when you are exhausted, and detaching from your technology when you get ready to sleep and when you first wake up.

I've been impressed seeing leaders such as Andrew Cuomo, gover-nor of New York, responding to the COVID-19 crisis by delivering clear, steady briefings day after day knowing he's probably incredibly sleep-deprived. When people are frightened during adversity, it's crucial for them to see their leaders as stable and unflappable. If your physical and mental stamina aren't strong, the people you lead will notice—and may lose confidence.

Emotional Capacity: Manage your reactions

Emotional capacity is how you react to challenging situations, your emotional mindset, and the quality of your relationships. It's vital for leaders to be emotionally resilient, but even more so in the face of challenging situations.

The leaders who are excelling now are the ones who are determined to control what they can control and focus on those who are depending on them, rather than acting from a place of fear. Building emotional capacity is essential to staying composed in a crisis and making clear-headed decisions under pressure.

Our relationships are also essential in times of crisis. These are the times to show the people who matter most to you that you value them. It's also likely to be a time where you'll learn which relationships in your life are most valuable and reciprocal.

Times of crisis are when we need and deserve the most from our leaders. In turn, leaders need to be prepared to rise to the occasion by building their capacity and refining their abilities in real time.

Capacity building isn't about doing more—it's about doing more of the right things. By building these four areas of capacity, you'll raise your game as a leader, help navigate a crisis, and put yourself and the people around you to be stronger long after this crisis is over.

Robert Glazer is the founder and CEO of Acceleration Partners, a premier global partner marketing agency. He is the author of the inspirational newsletter *Friday Forward*, the *Wall Street Journal* and *USA Today* best-seller *Elevate,* and the international best-selling book *Performance Partnerships*. He is also the host of the *Elevate Podcast.*

HOW TO REMOVE FEAR FROM YOUR WORK CULTURE

Adrian Gostick and Chester Elton

We all know that fear can get stuff done. If stress levels are amped up sufficiently, people can do some crazy things for short periods of time. We've all heard the story of the mom who lifts a car off a trapped family member. Marketers have long known the power of fear, using it to sell everything from life insurance to alarm systems to fiber cereals that taste like tree bark and feet.

A degree of fear in our workplaces is unavoidable with this pandemic and economic downturn. But it's important for leaders to recognize that fear at work can cause a host of ill effects that undermine the quality of people's output as well as overall team performance. At the heart of fear is doubt, and uncertainty can kill motivation, not to mention innovation.

When faced with a threat—real or imagined—the brain's amygdala sends out a distress signal, prompting the release of stress hormones, which cause physiological changes, including increased heartbeat, quickened breathing, and muscle tensing. This reaction is designed as a boon in response to immediate threats, giving us a surge of energy and enhancing our strength. *Shazam!* But all that is intended as a *temporary* response to danger, not as a prolonged state of being. As this pandemic worry stretches into weeks and months, it will sap energy. Chronic stress like that can also seriously undermine the quality of people's sleep, further undercutting their energy. Fear-induced stress is a major factor in burnout.

Getting people into a fight mode during a crisis might sound okay to some leaders: "they'll be charged up to tackle this challenge!" What they need to understand is that a fighting spirit, when evoked by fear rather than inspiration and a sense of purpose, can end up aimed right back against their managers instead of at the challenges to be tackled. Never underestimate the degree of bald-faced contempt that people let brew in response to the perception that a manager isn't doing all they can to solve the problems that are causing them to freak out (even if the manager has little to no control over them).

In short, few things in a crisis are worse than key stakeholders' perceiving leadership to be in disarray, indecisive, or indifferent. It is the very moment of crisis when the organization needs its people to believe the most, yet their faith is often challenged.

What to do as leaders? Here are a few tactics that can help.

Create a safe place

One sure-fire way to help reduce fear starts with frequently and honestly framing the market situation in real terms that people can relate to. Leaders must explain in clear terms what behaviors employees must focus their efforts on, all while creating a reassuringly safe environment to keep delivering to clients. During our interviews with leaders who successfully led their teams through the last global crisis, they displayed a dogged commitment to their mission and core values. Employees we interviewed later told us things like, "He forced us to keep thinking about our mission, and how we were helping make the world a better place," or "She reminded us that real people were using our products; they had to be perfect every time."

Leave the pillows at home

During tough times, it's more important than ever to be honest and transparent. In other words, don't soften the blow. Let people know what's up with the business in clear ways and communicate with them every day, even if there's not much to share. Part of this concept means you'll need to admit you need your employees' help and ideas to get through this. After all, you don't have all the ingenuity or improvement ideas in your head, so let your people know you want to hear their input. Encourage debate on ways to improve service or find new business or enhance processes, even if it rattles established harmony. When employees know their managers are seeking better ways during tough times, and are encouraging them to practice the same, it builds trust and a larger culture of optimism.

Amp up gratitude

It is in the worst of times that leaders must amp up praise and recognition of every step forward. In the organizations we studied that made it through the Great Recession in the best shape, there was a statistically significantly higher preponderance of gratitude of employee efforts than in those organizations that achieved average or poor returns. The seemingly warm and fuzzy skill of thanking people for the value they bring creates tangible feelings of hope and points people toward the right behaviors.

Manage to motivators

Every person on this planet has a thumbprint-like makeup of what makes them most engaged at work, and those prints vary considerably. During this stressful time, one of the most powerful ways to engage people is to align (as much as possible) assignments with a person's specific motivations and uncover subtle changes that can lead to increases in team morale, engagement, and results. The problem is, few managers know what's really motivating to their people or, if they do, how to apply that information to day-to-day work. The best leaders have discovered that the surest way to help their employees be more productive in challenging times is to do some sculpting of the nature of jobs or tasks to better match duties with passions.

Adrian Gostick and **Chester Elton** are the *New York Times* best-selling authors of *Leading with Gratitude*, *The Carrot Principle*, and *All In*. They own the global training company The Culture Works and work with organizations around the world to address employee engagement issues.

THE IMPORTANCE OF CEO SELF-CARE DURING PROLONGED CRISES

Shoma C. Hayden

Over the last ten years, ghSMART & Co., a leadership advisory firm, has conducted research on over 2,000 CEOs. The study, called CEO Genome,[1] uncovered an aspect of the job that often goes unspoken. While the CEO role comes with positional power, influence, wealth creation opportunities, and perks, it can also be a psychological thunder dome. CEOs face high-stake decisions, intense scrutiny of living in a fishbowl, and the need for 24×7 engagement with multiple stakeholders. Add to that the unrelenting nature of this multimonth "novel" pandemic, which can deplete the physical, psychological, and emotional reserves of CEOs (and their top teams).

We've spoken recently to some CEOs who have told us that they will "sleep when this is over and things are under control." They have morphed into "chief emergency officers" simultaneously triaging issues of liquidity, employee health, customer concerns, supply chain disruptions, and government interventions. We argue that this is the wrong

---

1. https://ceogenome.com/

time to eschew self-care. Conversely, the one thing utterly in a CEO's control right now is showing up in their absolute best condition to perform for themselves, their people, and the communities in which they operate.

Your brain in hyperdrive

The seminal *HBR* article[2] on CEO burnout in 1996, and subsequent decades of research in the field of "neuroleadership,"[3] have enhanced our understanding of our brain at work. Without a regimen to keep mind and body in fighting shape, the sustained exposure to the stresses of the chief emergency officer role can lead to an enlarged amygdala—the part of the brain that controls emotional reactions, and a weaker/thinner prefrontal cortex—the part of the brain responsible for cognitive functioning. The result: weaker attention spans, irritability, and social withdrawal, as well as decreased creativity, working memory, and problem-solving skills. A recent study[4] of 156 Swedish CEOs showed a notable correlation between a CEO's cognitive burnout in uncontrollable and sustained fight-or-flight conditions and lower firm performance.

While we have not faced a pandemic of this magnitude in our lifetimes, we can draw a few lessons from the 2008 financial crisis's impact on leaders; the most prominent example being that of Lloyds Banking Group CEO Antonio Horta-Osorio taking eight weeks off work to recover from the chronic and debilitating stress of the crisis. He later advocated for his senior team and employees to adopt measures to improve overall well-being.

A playbook for peak performance under high stress

Through observations and research, we offer seven strategies for leaders to improve renewal and resilience while market forces continue to gyrate.

---

2. https://hbr.org/1996/07/when-executives-burn-out
3. https://hbr.org/2010/04/leadership-on-the-brain
4. https://www.sciencedirect.com/science/article/pii/S0024630118300116

1. Draw strength from your value system. A leader's personal value system and identity can serve as a compass for making decisions in situations where there are no clear answers, only trade-offs (like cutting costs to stop the bleeding without damaging future prospects for growth; or guaranteeing no-layoff policies without knowing future financial position). As one executive prepared for another dizzying week of firefighting, a longitudinal reflection of her life and career—noting milestones, failures, successes, and aspirations—provided a sense of grounded-ness. The exercise helped her remember who she was, where she fits in the big picture, where she can make the most impact, and how she wants to be seen in one year, in five years, and in ten years. More importantly, reflecting on how she had overcome significant personal and professional hurdles in her life helped give her the conviction and strength to act more decisively today.

2. Commit to a regimen. Prolonged firefighting can hijack your ability to focus on longer-term, bigger-picture issues. Creating some sense of normalcy and routine help us reset—our brains function better when we take a break from complexity and sameness. Many leaders praise the benefits of meditative reflection,[5] which have been well documented by academics, hedge fund gurus, and wellness professionals. Whatever the regimen, it is important to stick to it, calendarize it, and find an accountability partner. As the CEO of Novartis shared in a recent *New York Times* article: "I have been working with a coach on four principles: mindset, movement, nutrition and recovery. . . . There's a feedback loop. If I build those four areas into my daily schedule, I have a bigger impact. So, I don't see it as making time. I just build it in."[6]

3. Sleep. While running executive development at Goldman Sachs, we heard from a number of thought leaders; perhaps the most in-

---

5. https://hbr.org/2020/03/why-leaders-need-meditation-now-more-than-ever

6. https://www.nytimes.com/2019/08/01/business/vas-narasimhan-novartis
-corner-office.html

triguing was Professor Jessica Payne, who highlighted the link between sleep and leadership. Sleep helps our brain commit information to memory and problem-solving. In fact, regions of the brain involved in learning, processing information, and emotion are *more* active during sleep than in waking hours. Our culture still applauds CEOs and other leaders who perform heroic feats of stamina and all-nighters. Interestingly, according to Dr. Charles Czeisler at Harvard Medical School, a week of sleeping four or five hours a night can induce impairment equivalent to a blood alcohol level of .1 percent. As counterintuitive as it sounds, sleep will in fact increase your productivity.

4. Monotask, don't multitask. Rather than multitasking, consider monotasking. Take a block of time to work only on one thing. Those in high-stress roles, such as soldiers tasked with disarming improvised explosive devices, will emphasize how staying in the moment and focusing on the task at hand is key to performance. When dealing with the pandemic is soaking up all your capacity, focus on doing one thing at a time. Have your leadership team follow similar principles.

5. Get energized doing what you love. Rediscover what you love (or used to love) about your job. When you don't have much time outside of work, this booster shot of energy can increase productivity and attention span. One CEO who rose through the ranks of sales and marketing derived energy from talking to customers; as a result, he took on the task of checking on the company's top twenty customers. Another found his flow in convening insurance industry colleagues to mount a joint response to aid those most vulnerable to the pandemic.

6. Resist the urge to withdraw. At a time of physical distancing, it is tempting to retreat to one's office to plow through the myriad demands on our time. The nature of the CEO job is lonely and peerless within a company. During crisis, however, the CEO should draw upon the counsel of key executive team members (the CFO being the prime example) as well as CEO peers in other companies and industries. Mining collective intelligence from diverse, informed sources improves the CEO's decision-making process and minimizes natural biases and blind spots. Relationships and social support are important coping mechanisms and a well-documented[7] precondition of well-being. The presence of positive social support reduces the likelihood of negative health outcomes in the wake of stressful events. Similarly, CEOs with coaches and advisers may conclude that this is the worst time for a coaching conversation. In fact, we have found that even a few minutes with an objective third party to vent, prioritize, and develop a plan to move forward, even for the upcoming week, can release the buildup of pressure and restore emotional modulation. These private conversations provide CEOs with a necessary, no-judgment emotional release so they can project calm when in public.

7. Experience the Helper's High. Turn outward and find ways to contribute to others, in ways big or small. At the onset of the pandemic, Microsoft's CEO sent an email[8] to the company's 140,000 employees thanking them and urging them to help others during the crisis: "For me, the best way I've found to get past this anxiety is to focus on what I can do each day to make a small difference." Like Satya Nadella, many CEOs are seizing the opportunity to leverage their company's assets and strengths—whether they be people, ideas, or infrastructure—to alleviate the crisis. In early March, LVMH quickly pivoted to turning its fragrance factories to produce hand sanitizers. Later in the month, Humana and Cigna waived patient copays on all treatment for coronavirus for their insured members. We have long known the PR benefits of corporate social giving, but studies[9] also show that it also boosts our physical and mental health.

CEO well-being may seem like a secondary or tertiary concern when so many others face food, health, and income insecurity. No doubt many CEOs are among the fortunate. However, their daily de-

7. https://psycnet.apa.org/record/1999-13139-006

8. https://www.seattletimes.com/business/microsoft-ceo-satya-nadella-to-employees-on-coronavirus-crisis-we-need-the-world-to-do-well/

9. https://health.clevelandclinic.org/why-giving-is-good-for-your-health/

cisions have multiplier effects on the lives and livelihoods of tens of thousands. Ensuring that they remain in the best possible shape to lead is always important, but it is paramount in times of crisis.

Shoma C. Hayden coheads ghSMART's Leadership Development and Coaching practice. She focuses on helping CEOs and their teams increase their collective resilience and performance.

LEADING BY INCLUSION WILL GET US THROUGH

Sally Helgesen

Until the virus upended our everyday existence, leaders tended to view inclusion as a nice-to-do thing primarily related to diversity. This isn't surprising, given how routine the pairing of D&I has become over the past decade. But diversity and inclusion are very different. Diversity describes the reality of today's global workforce. Inclusion describes the behaviors required to successfully lead a diverse workforce. Inclusion is thus the *precondition* for the full engagement of such a workforce. It is essential for convincing people with different backgrounds, experiences, and values that they belong, can have an impact, and will be valued for their potential as well as their contributions.

Inclusion may sound warm and fuzzy, but it requires facing two hard truths. First, that it can be demonstrated only by behaviors, not by mission statements or good intentions. Second, that inclusive behaviors must be demonstrated at the leadership level or they will have no real impact. Leaders who behave inclusively set the tone for the people they lead; if they hold others to account, these behaviors cascade down, creating an inclusive culture. Leaders who talk about "our commitment to inclusion" but fail to act inclusively also set the tone, while enabling those who view division as the route to power to shape the culture.

This is why inclusion cannot be outsourced to the D&I team, no matter how professional, expert, or well-led. Policies and programs do not shape culture. Ideas and stated commitments matter only if people see them being enacted at the top. Culture is always manifest in "how we do things." Recognizing this is essential during the present crisis, as people labor under extraordinary stress. Stress always tests systems and extreme stress has system-wide impacts, especially in organizations that lack resilience or in which trust is lacking. Inclusive practices are the only effective means of building trust and assuring resilience because only people who feel valued and seen by those who lead them are willing to trust their organizations.

How does a leader demonstrate inclusion and so build an inclusive culture? My thirty years of work with teams around the world make clear that three things are vital.

1. Recognize and support different kinds of power

The chief engineer and second hire at one of Silicon Valley's most storied companies once taught me a valuable lesson. I had asked him why his company was so good at eliciting strategic ideas from people at every level, which enabled them to make the most of their highly talented workforce (90 percent of their hires were engineers) and remain innovative even as the company grew huge and dominant.

His answer was simple. "It's because we recognize that in every organization there are four kinds of power. There's the power of position, where you stand in the hierarchy, always the most obvious kind of power. There's the power of personal authority, how your colleagues perceive and you, and especially the trust you inspire. There's the power of connections, who you know. And there's the power of expertise or *what* you know. Explicitly valuing all four types of power gives our people freedom to innovate no matter what their level. They don't need permission, they don't need to hold a specific position. So long as their idea sounds promising, we give them resources to test it. Which means a budget and access to others who can help."

The engineer pointed out that this kind of approach usually happens only when an organization is in its start-up phase, when lines of authority are loose and an all-hands-on-deck ethic prevails. Why? Because positional power becomes entrenched as an organization grows and command-and-control protocols are engaged to manage efficiencies. "As a result," said the engineer, "people—especially leaders—start believing that position is the only kind of power that matters. In a toxic culture, positional leaders resent and repress other kinds of power because they view it as a threat. They exclude others from important decision-making. Once that happens, you've created an exclusionary culture in which most people feel powerless to contribute."

2. Overlook nothing

The smallest gestures send a signal when you're trying to demonstrate inclusion. For example, I worked with the senior team at a global energy firm when a sector-wide commodity slide was decimating prices. The CEO was acutely aware of the stress his people were experiencing and worked hard to communicate that they mattered.

One day I visited his Houston office and was surprised to see an outward-facing sign on his desk: *Be Brief, Be Brilliant or Be Gone.* Since this message did not reflect the man I knew, I asked why he chose to display the sign. "Oh, that!" he answered. "Someone gave it to me. He thought it was funny, so I left it there." Did the CEO consider that it might be perceived as intimidating? "I never thought of that," he said. "It's certainly not what I intended."

Intentions count for little in terms of how people perceive you. This is especially true if you're in a position of power, in which case your people will always be trying to read you, ascribing meaning to your most casual words or actions. You want to make sure you do nothing careless to undercut what you're trying to communicate.

When I reminded the CEO of this, he said I was overblowing the importance of the sign. "I'm glad to remove it," he said, "but I doubt anyone has ever noticed." I asked if I might survey the people in his immediate area to find out. "Have at it," he responded, so I did. And I found that almost 70 percent of the people who had visited his office found it jarring, confusing, or alienating. As one noted, "I went in to see him because I had a suggestion, but when I read that I asked myself, is this brilliant? It wasn't, so I just kept my mouth shut."

3. Don't make exceptions for anyone who resists inclusive practices

Inclusion efforts most often fail because people in the ranks get a conflicting message from those to whom they directly report. Even when C-suite leaders articulate a strong commitment, those one or two levels down may be skeptical, especially if they perceive it as an HR or D&I initiative. As a result, they don't change their behavior and the people they lead don't get the message.

Holding senior people to account is difficult, especially if they are strong contributors. For example, I worked with the mining division of an Australian conglomerate that had undertaken a CEO-led initiative to try to expand the pool of talent from which the company drew by encouraging more inclusive behaviors at the senior level. Yet when the mining head announced the new policies at a team meeting, the supervisor of his exploration unit pushed back bluntly. "I'm not going in for this Mr. Inclusive b.s.," he said. "It's not my style. And since my division led our competitors for the last three years, I'm not about to change how we do things."

The head of mining was uncertain how to proceed. "This guy *is* one of the company's high performers and I don't want to send the message that we punish top-line producers if they don't immediately sign on to corporate initiatives." He said. "The guy is also very outspoken, and I could foresee him rallying people who disagree with the new approach, which would only make things more divisive."

The confusion and reluctance to deal with strong pushback this leader felt is common, but making exceptions for high performers sends the message to the entire organization that the commitment to inclusion is just a lot of talk that will have little impact upon how people really behave. Contrast his reluctance with the CEO of one of the world's largest manufacturers who called an all-hands meeting during his first week on the job. He told the assembled "generals and colonels" that he would be holding weekly meetings with them going forward, during which he would listen and address their concerns. He added that he was setting two ground rules for these meetings. First, no one would be permitted to trash anyone's ideas, as had been routine in the company. Second, there would be zero tolerance for backbiting and gossip.

The next day, the head of production with the highest numbers came to see him. "We don't really know each other yet," he said, "but I'm not one of these politically correct types who just falls into line. If I think someone in one of these meetings has a lousy idea, I'm going to let people know. And I don't appreciate being muzzled or told how to respond." The CEO smiled affably and said simply, "I understand how you feel. And I wish you luck in your new job with a different company. You've set a price for staying that we can't afford to meet."

The challenge of the moment is forcing all of us to consider what kind of practices will lead our organizations out of crisis and prepare for the uncertainty ahead. The outlook is still clouded, but one thing is sure: flexibility and innovation will be required from people at every level. And the only way to ensure this kind of robust and creative participation is to build cultures in which inclusive behaviors are expected and rewarded.

Sally Helgesen, cited in *Forbes* as the world's premier expert on women's leadership, is a bestselling author, speaker, and leadership coach. Her most recent book, *How Women Rise*, coauthored with coaching legend Marshall Goldsmith, became the top-selling title in its field within a week of publication.

CONNECTING WITH OUR HUMANITY IN ORDER TO THRIVE!

Terry Jackson

"I think that when the dust settles, we will realize how very little we need, how much we actually have, and the true value of human connection."—Unknown

In the middle of a crisis, it's hard to keep our worst fears at bay. Being jolted awake in a cold sweat at two in the morning with your mind spinning in fear is exhausting. Yet every leader knows these moments.

The noun crisis is the Latin form of the Greek word *krisis*, meaning "turning point, a critical moment." History is filled with nations, organizations, and leaders who have confronted profound crises, yet few can match the magnitude of the global pandemic we are currently facing.

Every crisis has two key components: leaders and the people they lead. While many succumb, some have found a way to help their teams *thrive* even in adversity. Nancy Koehn, author of *Forged in Crisis: The Power of Courageous Leadership in Turbulent Times*, shares the insights she gained by researching five leaders who triumphed despite almost unbeatable odds: polar explorer Ernest Shackleton marooned on an Antarctic ice floe; President Abraham Lincoln on the verge of the

Union's collapse; escaped slave turned abolitionist Frederick Douglass facing possible capture; Nazi-resisting clergyman Dietrich Bonhoeffer agonizing over how to counter absolute evil with faith; and environmental crusader Rachel Carson racing against the cancer ravaging her body in a bid to save the planet.

As they saw it, all these leaders were in the pursuit of making the world a better place for everyone. And each one, facing an impossible situation, was able to make smart, reasoned decisions despite the uncertainty and ambiguity confronting them. Equally important, they all made decisions that defied accepted wisdom.

Each leader was grounded in a desire to treat each person on their "team" as a valued human being. Each leader made it a priority to instill treating people with compassion and humanity as the essential principle of their time. Each leader fought to put an end to the objectification and dehumanization of individuals. And Koehn also reaches the inevitable conclusion that leaders are not born but *made,* opening us all to the realization that the power and courage to lead resides in *each* of us.

It is incumbent upon leaders everywhere to work tirelessly to end the constant objectification and dehumanization that pervades every aspect of today's society. It simply requires that we recognize all individuals as the human beings they are. No labels or titles—as this is one of the ways we dehumanize each other. "She is an engineer." "He is an attorney." "She is a criminal." "He is physically challenged." These descriptions and labels immediately give birth to biases, both conscious and unconscious, in the minds of others. Leaders must move away from these labels and simply call people by name to connect with their humanity; it is this human connection that will create an environment where everyone can *thrive.*

Just as flowers and trees grow through concrete, humans, too, grow through adverse conditions. Each leader's mandate should be to create an environment in which a determination and ability to *thrive* is embedded in the DNA of every individual. In fact, we should not rest until it becomes part of "natural law" in the twenty-first century.

To this end, leaders must do what it takes so that every individual in their sphere of influence can *thrive*. This requires that leaders be Transparent, practice Humility, exemplify Respect and Resilience, have profound Insight, see Vulnerability as a strength that connects them to the people they lead, Encourage all to seek continuous improvement and growth, and finally, Engage everyone in the importance and value of creating a culture where everyone can *thrive*.

Reflecting on the moments of crisis faced by Douglass, Lincoln, Shackleton, Bonhoeffer, and Carson, they all displayed a measure of *transparency*, not only with their supporters but also with those who opposed them. Each summoned *humility* and used it as a position of strength as they embraced their crisis. *Respect* was also a trait that each leader either possessed or mastered while in crisis. Driven by purpose larger than themselves, these leaders were also able to draw on their *resilience* as they struggled to confront the challenges they faced.

Insight was also a critical gift these extraordinary leaders relied on as they struggled to triumph over the adversities they faced, and they used their *vulnerability* to enhance their humanity. It was also each leader's awareness that enabled them to be continuously be *encouraged* by the progress they were making.

All these leadership traits together enabled these five gifted leaders to *engage* both their advocates and their opponents on the darkest of days, and gain buy-in to their overarching vision for humanity that enabled them to successfully lead through the crises they were facing. They were able to *thrive* by understanding the importance of the human element.

As we enhance our understanding of human nature, we learn an important truth: leaders come in all shapes and sizes. Many school librarians are wonderful leaders who shape children's lives in immeasurable ways. Many firefighters and chemo nurses are also extraordinary leaders who save lives and give people hope during times of crisis. And we can all name CEOs who have built successful, humane organizations that put making a positive difference on a par with generating profits for their shareholders.

Today we face a crisis of monumental proportions. As our collective disillusionment with our nation's leaders grows, so, too, does our search for authentic leaders in other places and other roles, leaders who know how to create an environment where everyone can *thrive*. The call to lead with integrity and honor has never been louder than it is today. Leadership and collectivism are essential if we are to be citizens of the universe and successfully navigate in a world where we have minimized people's ability to *thrive*.

Until we all connect to our own humanity and the humanity of others, we will not *thrive* as a collective. Until we eradicate the objectification and dehumanization of others, we will not connect as members of the human race.

It is time for us all to begin to take responsibility for improving our own lives and the world in which we live. It is time to value our differences as a source of strength rather than divisiveness. It is time we all stand up and begin contributing and constructing rather than denouncing and destroying. It is time to come together in a spirit of shared purpose and commitment to our collective humanity.

It is time to build upon our strengths and develop our weaknesses. It is time that we recognize and celebrate the human spirit and tap into this incredible source of unlimited potential, redirecting our energy, time, and efforts toward more constructive and meaningful purposes.

It is time for all of us to embrace the transformational thinking that will enable us all to *thrive*!

Dr. Terry Jackson is an executive advisor, thought leader, and organizational consultant. Terry is a Marshall Goldsmith 100 Coaches. Terry was recently chosen by Thinkers50 as one of the top fifty Leaders in Coaching. Terry was chosen by Thinkers360 as a top fifty thought leader in the Future of Work.

KEEP PLANTING CHERRY TREES

Whitney Johnson

We find ourselves in uncharted waters.

A pandemic, political wrangling, a volatile stock market indicating economic harm. We've experienced most of this before, in some form or another, but right now it seems like we've sailed our ship into a Bermuda Triangle of uncertainty and chaos.

These macro events coupled with the micro anxieties that accompany our everyday human lives might make us fear that we are sinking. There's no question that this crisis has been disconcerting, and that our concerns continue to snowball and accelerate. But as novel as the novel coronavirus is, there is nothing new about trouble and challenge. When we succumb to fear and the paralysis or overreaction that it can stimulate, we are more likely to abandon the ship than to have it simply sink on its own.

Take the stock market, for example. I find myself sympathetic to stories of folks emptying their accounts and stuffing their money under a mattress. The truth is, we who invest decide what will happen to the market. Will the market continue to drop precipitously? If we liquidate our positions and stuff our money under the mattress, it will. If we invest, it will recover and climb.

To paraphrase economist John Maynard Keynes, the social object of investment is to defeat fear.

That fear, I believe, is fear of the future, and even in some ways, fear of the unknown present. Should we throw caution to the wind? No, of course not. But should we stop investing? To do so seems tantamount to thinking that the future is not just uncertain; it simply doesn't exist. There is no future.

A little drastic. The future has always been uncertain. If WWI accompanied by the Spanish influenza of 1918–19, followed a decade later by the Great Depression, and then yet another, even more destructive, world war didn't sink the human ship, I see no reason to believe today's stormy waters will. We can abandon it. But let's not.

Said more pithily, and paraphrasing western colonizer Brigham Young, we need to keep planting cherry trees.

History is a great instructor. We need to be more historically minded—for our own good. History teaches us that the human family has risen to hard challenges—repeatedly—with a combination of hard work, courage, and ingenuity. Those tools are our legacy from our ancestors as much as levers, wheels, and pulleys are. We've been disrupted, but we've kept turning the lessons learned from difficulty and loss to our future advantage for millennia.

I don't want to minimize the impact of these disruptions on individual lives and families. Hard and even tragic things are happening to people. None of us are completely insulated from consequential discomfort and harm.

One defining feature of a crisis, it seems to me, is a sudden contraction of resources. We all are conscious of scarcity these days. We can see that our grocery market's shelves are less stocked. The portfolios represented by the stock market are less funded, and revenue streams for smaller businesses have diminished to a trickle. There are fewer jobs and less income. Most critically, there are sometimes not enough ventilators, hospital beds, face masks, and other PPE. It is symbolic of the entire COVID-19 pandemic that we all know what PPE is; most of us were unfamiliar with the abbreviation until recently. Now discussion of its scarcity dominates public discourse.

Scarcity is at the root of our fear of the future. It can also fuel a self- and community-defeating level of competition, as with the fifty individual states of the United States pitted against one another and against the national government, racing to acquire sufficient medical resources in anticipation of the coronavirus crisis' hitting home. New York State, where the pandemic's full fury was felt first and worst in the US, begged for ventilators. Some were forthcoming, but not nearly enough. New York governor, Andrew Cuomo, daily solicited additional supplies, explaining that New York would need them first, but not exclusively. Send New York your ventilators for our crisis, he continually exhorted, and we will send them to other states when their critical moment arrives. Resources are meant to be used.

When resources are scarce, sharing them, rather than competing for them, is our best policy. Maybe it always is. But this is especially a time for us to be looking for ways to share the wins, even if they are individually smaller, rather than go for the big win ourselves at the expense of others. Thomas Troward said, "Life ultimately consists in *circulation*, whether within the physical body of the individual or on the scale of the entire solar system; circulation means a continual flowing around." An early lesson of the COVID-19 pandemic is that we need to keep limited resources circulating and at work. Hoarding serves the few, but it doesn't serve humanity. Selling all our positions in the stock market may save us from some individual loss, but it undermines the entire economy to the ultimate detriment of all, including ourselves. The only thing that helps us is to continue to invest—in the present and the future.

Besides financial, what form can those investments take? What cherry trees can we plant? I advocate that whether in "normal" times we are proactively disrupting ourselves, or we have been disrupted by an unanticipated crisis, we must embrace our constraints if we are to prosper. Constraints are, by definition, limitations on resources. My mentor, Clayton Christensen, claimed that the Great Recession a decade ago would have an unmitigated positive impact on innovation because, when resources are the most limited, the tension is greatest, and people are forced to rethink the way they do business. Rethinking results in innovation. Because of the Great Recession and the innovations it required, we have more resources to stay connected, continue working, make informed decisions, and support one another than at any time in the past.

Rethink the future. During the recession, when available jobs were constrained, many found that it was a good time to go back to school for additional education and a new credential. That may be a wise investment for many in this and future crises. During the last recession, the gig economy was born and entrepreneurship skyrocketed. The present demands rethinking of how those trends need to develop to serve both workers and customers in the future. The same is true of enterprises in the shared economy—Uber, Lyft, Airbnb, and so forth. Subscription businesses will need to evolve to adapt to consumers who have fewer resources and are more vigilant about recurring expenses. Rather than focusing on this as a season of scarcity, we should invest in it as a season of opportunity.

The Kauffman Foundation reported in 2009[1] that 51 percent of Fortune 500 companies began during a recession or bear market or both. Historically, most successful start-ups beg in vain for funding. I highlight the stories of a lot of immigrants in my podcast. Why? Because immigrants are more than twice as likely to start a business as native-born Americans. About 40 percent of the Fortune 500 were founded by immigrants or their children. These are people who have often left all behind—homes, businesses, support networks of families and friends and professional associates. Sometimes they do so proactively, but often they are forced by crisis, as we are now, to disrupt themselves. They plant cherry trees and create a successful life out of virtually nothing.

We are in unfamiliar territory. It's time to think like an immigrant, embrace our constraints, and confront and defeat our fears by investing in the future.

It will affect everything we do and are. And our children. Our children's children. There will be opportunities for new growth; if we look for those and embrace even the everyday constraints (can't travel,

---

1. https://www.kauffman.org/wp-content/uploads/2009/06/theeconomicfuture justhappened.pdf

must telecommute, lost half the budget, have to start again in a new place or start a new business entirely, etc.), we will emerge from this historic moment better prepared for the challenges of the future. Which *will* come. Let's keep living, preparing, disrupting, and innovating to meet those challenges.

Said Sarah Ban Breathnach "Both abundance and lack exist simultaneously in our lives, as parallel realities. It is always our conscious choice which secret garden we will tend."

Innovation is the happy fruit of the resourcefulness demanded by hard times.

Keep planting cherry trees.

Whitney Johnson is one of fifty leading business thinkers globally (Thinkers50), and the #1 Talent Coach—Marshall Goldsmith Leading Global Coaches. A cofounder of the Disruptive Innovation Fund with Harvard's Clayton Christensen, Johnson wrote the award-winning *Disrupt Yourself* (Harvard Business Press) and is a LinkedIn *Top Voice* with 1.8 million followers.

TO CONQUER A CRISIS, LEADERS BUILD TRUST

Tom Kolditz

Whether you are a formal leader in an organization, or you're just try-ing to lead as a congregant in your church or a member of your family, a significant personal or professional crisis will eventually catch up to you. With no conscious choice, you are now an *in extremis* leader. *In extremis* leadership (*in extremis* is Latin for "at the point of death") is influencing people under conditions where leader decisions can affect peoples' physical well-being or survival. *In extremis* leadership is taught to new leaders in our military service academies, specifically Air Force and Army, and in other military schools around the world, including the Israel Defense Force Military Psychology Center and the Japanese National Defense Academy. The concept is based on research done in Iraq in the early 2000s, and with military and civilian leaders at West Point. The principles inherent to leading people who are afraid are important, because what people need from their leaders changes in times of deep concern. And every one of us, in the course of our life-long journey, will unfortunately have to live and work with people who are afraid, for their lives, or their lifestyle and livelihood. It all pivots on trust.

To be clear, these principles for maintaining trust in crisis are as important when there is a crisis in business contexts as when there is a physical threat. As we began to study leadership in dangerous contexts, we assumed that the resultant lessons would be reserved for those in physically threatening circumstances—soldiers, mountain climbing guides, law enforcement, firefighters, and similar physically dangerous occupations. Then one day, a group of investment bankers visited us at West Point. I assured them that our work, while interesting, really didn't apply to them. Fifteen minutes into the presentation, I was challenged by one of the investment bankers who told harrowing stories of the loss of money, and how it powerfully impacted her and her friends. As a result, our research team worked hard to determine if actual physical risk was relevant, or merely deeply felt fear, helplessness, and anger—whether or not there was physical threat. As it turns out, the response of a person to a threat to their lifestyle or livelihood is indeed deeply felt. People experiencing such emotions are seeking precisely the same things from their leaders as soldiers who experience such emotions on the battlefield, or a mountain climber on a dangerous climb. These principles apply to your ability to lead in crisis, whether the threat is physical or not.

The first principle we uncovered is called *inherent motivation*. Under threat, people are already aroused, even when they don't outwardly show it. Therefore, *in extremis* leaders have to avoid energetic cheerleading, or showing fear, or anger. It's a challenge for many leaders who, in more routine times, feel that they have to inject excitement or enthusiasm into a group. People need a calming influence, not a motivating influence, when under threat. They are distrustful of leaders who spin them up—because they sense the crisis may become worse, and if the leader is already animated, where will they be when things are even worse?

The second principle of *in extremis* leadership is *outward orientation*. Leaders should adopt a focus on the challenges of their work and the externals that are threatening them, because such focus mutes the emotions of fear or anger. The best leaders can create the same focus in the people around them. In addition to muting unproductive emotions, outward orientation is terrific for problem solving and learning. It creates the conditions for people to come up with creative, breakthrough solutions to problems, so now is not the time to ease up on anyone. Gently push them to focus on solutions. They will come through for you.

Third, *in extremis* leaders demonstrate *shared risk*. People trust those who lead from the front. Leaders need to show that they have "skin in the game," and ensure that they know when it comes time to demonstrate courage: for example, to leave the house to pick up food during a pandemic, or to face angry and irate clients or stakeholders as a business is struggling. It's the leader who must step up. Leaders who shrink from personal risk relative to those they are leading are not worthy of trust.

Next, leaders need to show a *common lifestyle* with the people they lead. People want to feel socially closer to their leaders when under threat, because people feel less concern about leaders throwing them under the bus in a furlough or for the mere convenience of the company. I once had a client whose employees lost homes in a storm send his staff a selfie of his airplane that overturned in the gale—his people, we learned, had never felt more distant. Executive leaders fleeing to their vacation homes while their employees tough it out in the trenches during a hurricane or pandemic is a sad iconic image. Leaders who do that are literally leaving their people behind, and will need to repair a significant decrease in trust with the rank and file as a result.

The final research finding was a special relationship between the *competence* of the leader and *loyalty* shown to others. Under threat, people's focus on leader confidence skyrockets. They have to believe that their leaders' decisions are in their best interest, as well as that of the company. It's so pronounced, that people who used to be collaborative often change, and they just want a strong, competent leader to tell them exactly what to do. In order for this shift to occur, the leader must be viewed as highly competent, and worthy of trust because of their demonstrated loyalty to the people who work with them. Competence includes confidence projected by calm, and by a history of people seeing the leader make good decisions. Loyalty is created by authentic concern for others. Leaders who lack either quality will be ineffective in influencing others who are under threat.

We will always live and lead in challenging times. Few of us will traverse our journey free of difficulty, tragedy, even horrific experiences. In some ways, though, people are even more ready to be organized and united than before they've become afraid. Give some thought to how you are influencing others as a leader, teammate, or family member. You'll be in a much better position when the crisis abates.

Brig. Gen. Tom Kolditz is the founding director of the Ann and John Doerr Institute for New Leaders at Rice University, and led the Department of Behavioral Sciences and Leadership at West Point for twelve years. He is the author of *In Extremis Leadership: Leading as if Your Life Depended on It.*

TWO PRINCIPLES FOR LEADING YOUR ORGANIZATION THROUGH THE COVID-19 CRISIS

Harry M. Kraemer

The challenges facing organizations, employees, and communities in the COVID-19 crisis are unprecedented, the stakes are high, and certainty is nowhere to be found. Under such staggering circumstances, it is only natural for leaders to feel unprepared to lead capably, nimbly, and honorably.

"You're feeling worry, fear, anxiety, pressure, and stress. And these feelings completely overwhelm you. And as a result of basically becoming overwhelmed, you almost become incapacitated," says Harry Kraemer.

Kraemer is a former chairman and CEO of the $12 billion global healthcare company Baxter International. In addition to being a clinical professor of leadership at Kellogg, he also is an executive partner with the private equity firm Madison Dearborn. Over the years, he has led through crises small and large—including a tragic crisis involving faulty dialyzers and patient deaths.

In his view, there are two main things leaders need to understand in a crisis—two mantras, if you will, that offer a calm way forward, no matter what the situation. And, as he has been cautioning boards and management teams repeatedly in the past few weeks, COVID-19 is no exception.

"Almost every crisis is different. So there's not a game plan for solving the crisis. However, there is a game plan, in my mind, for how you should approach the crisis," he said.

Mantra 1: You're going to do the right thing, and you're going to do the best you can do

It sounds deceptively simple, so say it again. And again. You're going to do the right thing. You're going to do the best you can do.

After all, that's all you can do.

Of course, that's much more difficult than it sounds, Kraemer acknowledged. You don't have to figure out what "the right thing" is all on your own. Nobody is smart enough or superhuman enough for that. Instead, surround yourself with people whom you trust and whose values align with yours and with those of the organization. Collectively, you will determine the right thing—and then do your best to act on it.

Picture your absolute worst nightmare, he said. For him, it would be learning that a member of his family had become critically ill with the virus; for others, it might be something quite different. Regardless, the way forward is clear: "I'm going to do the right thing, and with a lot of people's help, I'll do the best I can do," he said. "I try to repeat this over and over again. Worry, fear, anxiety, pressure, and stress can be significantly reduced."

And by the way, he said, if you start off trying to do the right thing and it turns out it's the wrong thing, you can adjust. Ego should be removed from the decision-making process; changing your mind is encouraged! "As I told a board earlier today, we're not trying to be right; we're trying to do the right thing," Kraemer said.

So what does following this mantra look like in practice—particularly when an organization's values might conflict around, say, serving the community, prioritizing safety, and practicing fairness?

"Say I've got a company with 100 employees," Kraemer said. "And fifty of them are in cubicles, but fifty of them are literally making the product and they're on an assembly line on the plant floor. Then COVID-19 happens. What's the right thing?"

For the fifty people in cubicles, you may send them home, even if it isn't strictly fair: it will protect them and make the people on the assembly line safer as well. For the other fifty employees, the decision is harder. Do you need to continue to manufacture at all? If so—perhaps you're making masks or hospital supplies or other essentials—are there ways to make the process safer, perhaps by extending the manufacturing line so people can work farther apart?

"That may mean we don't make as many products. Maybe that means we're not as efficient. Maybe that means our costs go up. But that's something we should do because we want to protect our people," he said.

Above all, be upfront about these trade-offs, as well as the risk to your employees. "I think what a value-based leader does is not only acknowledge that there is an elephant in the room," he said. "They turn the floodlights on so everyone can clearly see the elephant."

Mantra 2: You're going to tell people what you know, what you don't know, and when you'll get back to them to discuss what you didn't know before

As the contours of the crisis become clearer, the exact communications will obviously change. But the general format will look the same: you're going to tell people what you know, what you don't know, and when you'll get back to them to discuss what you didn't know before.

The first part, telling people what you know, is straightforward. For COVID-19, this might require gathering data about your own operations, as well as learning as much as you possibly can about the virus, and the federal, state, and community responses to it. Then, share this information as simply and honestly as you possibly can, even if it is not what people want to hear.

The second part—letting people know what you don't know—tends to be even more difficult for leaders. "People will say, well, I don't know if I want to get everybody together and let them know what I don't know," Kraemer said.

But telling people what you don't know is the key to building credibility with your stakeholders, he explained. Omit this step, and customers, employees, and others will recognize you aren't being upfront with them and might assume that you can't be trusted or the truth is more nefarious than it really is.

"You're not giving the people an understanding of what you're doing and why, so it looks like you're just jerking everything around and you lose all credibility."

Finally, you will need to tell people how quickly you'll get back to them with any outstanding questions they may have. "We don't know the answer to that issue yet, but here's what we're going to do: we'll have another conference call or we'll send out an email tomorrow with an update on what we didn't know yesterday," Kraemer said.

Adhering to this mantra isn't just about helping others, either, he said. It's a good strategy for protecting your own reputation and that of your organization. Without this level of communication, "you're not giving the people an understanding of what you're doing and why, so it looks like you're just jerking everything around and you lose all credibility. And that lack of trust creates chaos." People will start to think, "Either I'm being lied to, or the people in charge are idiots."

Beyond reputation, the mantra also offers an organizing framework to keep the entire organization on track. "The process, I think, has an enormous impact on how you operate as an organization and how you help the organization not get frozen in place with everybody running around like crazy," he said.

A failing during the current crisis, in Kraemer's view, is that too many leaders, including many in the government, haven't been upfront about the nature of the crisis: exactly what they know, all the things that they don't, and how they plan to seek additional information and provide citizens with updates in the future.

The worst-case scenario, he said, is one where people are truly surprised by how events are unfolding. You can't eliminate surprise, of course, but with strong communication and follow-through, you can minimize it.

Putting it all together

Leaders who follow these two mantras closely stand the best chance of emerging from the current crisis with their conscience—and their organization—intact.

Some companies and industries are already handling the crisis in ways that will reflect well on them in the future, Kraemer said. The airlines are bending over backward to allow people to cancel or change flights without incurring fees, for instance, while Major League Baseball clubs have pledged $30 million to the thousands of ballpark employees who will lose income while the league is on hiatus.

"It may hurt your profitability in the short term, but the long-term impact is going to be very, very positive because they did the right thing," Kraemer said.

Harry M. Jansen Kraemer, Jr. is an executive partner with Madison Dearborn Partners, a private equity firm based in Chicago, Illinois and a clinical professor of leadership at Northwestern University's Kellogg School of Management. He was named a Kellogg School Professor of the Year. Harry is the author of two bestselling leadership books: *From Values to Action: The Four Principles of Values-Based Leadership* and *Becoming The Best: Build a World-Class Organization Through Values-Based Leadership.* Harry's third book, *Your 168: Finding Purpose & Satisfaction in a Values-based Life* will be published in May 2020.

He is the former chairman and chief executive officer of Baxter International Inc., a $12 billion global healthcare company.

BECOME THE LEADER YOU WANT TO BE

Hortense le Gentil

With the entire world flying on the same plane, we are collectively facing an unprecedented time of turbulence and are in a state of shock. The oxygen masks have come down. How should you react to this situation? How can you take care of the individuals around you? Your colleagues? Your family? What is the best way to react?

I have three suggestions that will hopefully help you be the best leader you can be:

1. Hit the 'pause button'

As we are instructed by flight attendants, we must put on our own oxygen masks first.

Here are a few things you can do:

- Reclaim your mental space and find ways to refuel.
- Be present in the moment.
- Take a step back and reconnect with yourself.
  - What are your values?
  - What drives you and why?
  - Who are you?
- Go back to your Role Models. How did they act in times of uncertainty?

2. Be the best version of yourself

Try these tools to stay aligned and authentic:

- Stay calm and confident. One step after the other.
- Feed your own power by adopting a positive attitude.
- Focus on what you can change and impact, and let go of what is not in your control.
- Listen to your intuition, your best guide in uncertain times.

3. Create a safe space for your team

Feeling safe is the most basic human need. It is being challenged by the current crisis. Here are some potential actions to help with this:

- Communicate with your staff every day. Do this consistently *at the same time each day*. It will create a routine that will reassure your team. Your team will know that you are in charge and that your priority is them.
- Maintain "eye contact" as much as possible. Use video conferencing. People who are working from home will appreciate keeping a social "working environment." Moreover, eye contact can help maintain the link between people and create a safe place.
- Ask your managers to do the same with their teams. You will facilitate the "alignment of alignments."
- Apply this to your family as well, if they are far away from you. Set up a "family team."
- Set up helpline/channels such as Skype or Gmail chats where your colleagues can help one another.

All this may help you keep your community connected, aligned, and focused.

Hortense le Gentil is passionate about helping business leaders reach greater professional and personal success by aligning their personal values and professional activities. She is the author of *Aligned: Connecting*

Your True Self with the Leader You're Meant to Be. Her coaching is informed by her thirty years in business, working across a number of industries—including media consulting, advertising, technological innovation, and entrepreneurship.

CONNECT DURING CRISIS

Michelle Tillis Lederman

Since the start of the twenty-first century we have experienced four major crises: the bubble burst of dotcoms and telecoms, 9/11, the sub-prime mortgage collapse leading to the global financial crash of 2008, and the COVID-19 pandemic in 2020.

It is only natural for people, leaders, and their teams, to feel stressed in times of crisis. That stress reaction impacts your behavior in multiple ways, including amplifying your communication tendencies, triggering your fight-or-flight response, and prompting fear-based decision-making.

One powerful way to reduce our stress reaction is through connection. Under typical circumstances, the evidence tying your well-being to your connections is abundant. Research shows that strong social connections strengthen your immune system, reduce stress hormones, and increase dopamine, which produces the sensation of pleasure.[1] Connections don't just feel good—they are good for us.

Relationships also impact our happiness on the job. According to the *Journal of Applied Psychology*, close work friendships boost em-

---

1. Emma M. Seppälä, "Connect to Thrive," *Psychology Today*, August 26, 2012, https://www.psychologytoday.com/us/blog/feeling-it/201208/connect -thrive.

ployee satisfaction by 50 percent and predict happiness at work.[2] Crisis gives us an opportunity to connect on a deeper level with those we work with. Leaders who take this opportunity and create a Connected Culture in the organization during times of difficulty will see the impact post-crisis. **Connected Leadership** creates loyalty, increases productivity, and reduces turnover of talent. Organizations and individuals earn loyalty by the way they treat people in the bad times. Connected leaders understand that the greatest assets organizations have are their people.[3]

A **Connected Leader** needs to do two things; 1) show their people they care about them as people, and 2) show their people they care about the things they care about. When they do this consistently and uniformly, they create a **Connected Culture**. During a crisis, these two ideas are critically important and are applicable on both the personal and professional front. There are many ways to implement these ideas.

Be vulnerable and share your emotions

This is not the time to put on a front. Open up to your employees about how the crisis is affecting you personally and how you are processing the uncertainty in the situation. When you are willing to be vulnerable, it gives those around you a sense of permission to not just have similar feelings but also a willingness to share those emotions.

Taking the lead and revealing vulnerability establishes a climate of psychological safety, coined by Harvard professor Amy Edmondson as "a team climate characterized by interpersonal trust and mutual respect in which people are comfortable being themselves."[4]

---

2. Christine M. Riordan, "We All Need Friends at Work," *Harvard Business Review*, July 3, 2013, https://hbr.org/2013/07/we-all-need-friends-at-work.

3. Michelle Tillis Lederman, *The Connector's Advantage: 7 Mindsets to Grow Your Influence and Impact* (Page Two Books, 2019).

4. Amy Edmondson, "Psychological Safety and Learning Behavior in Work Teams," *Administrative Science Quarterly* 44, no. 2 (June 1999): 350.

Check in personally

Show you care about your people beyond their work product even more during a crisis. Phrase questions that assume the stress and worry exists, so people don't feel compelled to present a strong front. Such as, "How are you handling the _____?" And be willing to answer the same question in return. Probe beyond the basics and express concern for their family and life. If you worry about dredging up all the negative feelings, intersperse positively framed questions. For example, "How are you having fun/finding happiness during _____?" or "What have been your silver linings in the situation?"

Learning about what your team's interests are and who and what they care about outside of the office will create greater connection once the event is over. The sharing brings people together. The knowledge gained allows people to be more connected to each other and the team.

Communicate constantly

Crisis is a time of uncertainty and constant change. A lack of communication breeds unease. As a result, trust and psychological safety can quickly erode. Communicate constantly, even when you don't have anything concrete to say. Sharing, even when you don't have the answers, builds confidence and a sense of common experience. Communicate the information you can and explain what and why you can't reveal and when you hope to be able to.

As written in *The Connector's Advantage*: "Transparent leadership is key to creating a culture of trust between leaders and their employees. When employees are kept in the loop and understand their role in the overarching purpose and goals, they are more engaged and have greater trust in their employer." Be visible, accessible, and keep people in the loop even if you don't have all the answers, and they will trust that you will tell them when you do.

Connect to purpose

In the best of times, people want to have a sense of purpose. It is even more relevant during a crisis when everything can feel out of control.

Finding purpose helps put events in perspective and refocus energy on action. It is grounding. Taking action together creates shared purpose, shared experience, and shared community as well as a greater sense of control over the uncertainty. Purpose can be found both in and outside the organization.

Internally, what was a common understanding of priorities and activities may now seem irrelevant. A shared sense of purpose is foundational to the team and company culture as it defines what you are trying to achieve. Reassess, redirect if appliable, and evolve the understanding of the common goals.

Explain the *why* behind the *what* of the work and how it has changed as a result of current events and how it is still relevant. Take the purpose beyond the job and into the community. Providing opportunities for people to be in service, support a cause, and come together with a shared mission and value solidifies the connection beyond the crisis.

Create group practices

As a leader, implementing or continuing group activities during crisis can not only maintain connection but deepen it. Crisis is not the time to cut habits that were established for a reason. Create community, try:

Gratitude sharing. At the start of a meeting you can ask each person to share something they are grateful for. Often in a crisis there are some surprising silver linings. During the coronavirus pandemic lockdown, the world has seen a positive impact on the environment.

Meditation and mindfulness. Already used regularly in business to boost emotional intelligence, these practices are also believed to reduce stress and anxiety and increase resilience. Try starting a team meeting with a guided meditation to help ground and align your team.

Social gatherings. Don't cancel the happy hour or holiday party in times of crisis, just readjust what it looks like. During the pandemic, virtual happy hours (drinks included) have been a regular occurrence.

Crisis can come in many forms. In these times, we can feel detached and aimless. Reducing emotional isolation, creating common purpose, and staying connected to one another personally and professionally is critical. When people, teams, and organizations connect during crisis, they emerge even stronger.

Michelle Tillis Lederman, CSP, has written four books, including *The 11 Laws of Likability* and *The Connector's Advantage*. A speaker, trainer, and coach, she is CEO of Executive Essentials, which provides communications and leadership programs. A former finance executive and NYU professor, she is a frequent media contributor and holds degrees from Lehigh University and Columbia Business School.

THE DISRUPTION MINDSET: FINDING THE OPPORTUNITIES IN DISRUPTION

Charlene Li

Some leaders and their organizations thrive on disruption. When times are calm, they intentionally stir things up to find hidden nuggets for growth. And during turbulent times, they jump in with both feet, confident in their ability to come out okay on the other side.

These leaders have what I call a disruption mindset. They don't think of disruption as negative or something to avoid. Instead, they believe that *disruption creates opportunities for change.* That's because when a disruption happens, our sense of normal is torn into pieces and thrown into the air. The people who thrive with disruption jump into the air to catch the pieces before they fall. Those who instead duck their heads and hope not to get hit become victims of disruption.

Finding opportunities amid the disruption

In a downturn, it's natural to double down on your existing and best customers, making sure they have everything and hopefully ensuring your organization's continued sustainability. But focusing only on your existing customers limits your opportunities for growth. During disruptive times, needs don't go away—they shift and if you miss them, competitors and new entrants will gain a competitive advantage over you.

Many organizations fall prey to an innovation paradox: When times are flush and cash is plentiful, it's hard to take risks and there's a fear of failure. After all, why try something new when things are working well? When times are tough, it's easier to make risky bets because you've got nothing to lose, but resources are hard to come by.

Overcoming the innovator's dilemma

Organizations have a lot going for them, from brand and talent to scale and cash. But they also have existing customers who can become an anchor in a recession, keeping incumbent companies from exploring new growth areas.

In contrast, start-ups have nothing except the most important thing during disruptive times—the ability to look freely for the emerging future customers. Unencumbered by existing customers, they gain a foothold where no one else would think or want to go. This was the biggest issue that Professor Clayton Christensen identified as the "innovator's dilemma"—the unwillingness and inability of incumbents to chase after unprofitable, emerging customers.

It's so easy to be blinded by our profitable customers—and so fail to see the opportunities emerging on the edges. Disruptive leaders do this so well—they put on their disruption goggles to focus on opportunities to change and grow. They still treat their existing customers well, but they know that growth likely lies elsewhere.

Several things developed over the past decade that flipped this dynamic. Organizations can now identify future customers because of better tools that capture and analyze the voice of the customer via digital and social connections. Enterprise collaboration tools use artificial intelligence to get the knowledge of that future customer quickly to the right people in the organization who can act. And greater workforce empowerment and connection means that frontline employees closest to the customers can get heard by people in the C-suite.

Develop a disruption mindset by focusing on future customers

One thing that disruptive leaders do better than anything else is to relentlessly focus on the needs of customers in the future, constantly looking for opportunities for exponential change and growth. Disruptive leaders look at things counterintuitively. During flush times, they challenge their organizations to disrupt the status quo, paranoid that what works today won't work tomorrow. And during bad times, they accelerate their investments for the future because they know that's where the growth will be.

They know that in times of disruption, needs don't go away: they shift. And if you can shift with the need, you can fill the gap. Organizations and leaders that thrive with disruption can better sense and act on those opportunities because they were already doing this *before* the chaos hit. But it's not too late!

The forced pivot toward a more digitally connected workforce has been difficult for many people, but it has laid the foundation for a more flexible and agile organization capable of capitalizing on disruptive opportunities. We are in the early days of this next economic cycle, but I remain hopeful that organizations and their leaders are better equipped to focus on the needs of future customers today than ever before.

Here are five things you can do to develop your disruption mindset:

1. Be paranoid and prepared. As the Latin proverb says, "Fortune favors the prepared mind." Disruptive leaders don't pretend to know what the future will be like—but they are paranoid that what worked in the past will likely not work in the future. Use scenario planning to model out the most likely future paths and to practice the rigor of anticipating alternative, less likely paths. Prepare for multiple iterations of the future, confident in your knowledge that your organization can flex and adapt as needed.

2. Invest in structure and process. It seems counterintuitive, but the most disruptive organizations are actually high functioning with clear structure and process. The key is that the governance is finely tuned to support disruptive growth, laying out how work gets done so that people can focus all their energy on *getting* work done. For example, Amazon's innovation process uses a highly structured "press release from the future" and six-page FAQ. Make it clear how information will be shared, how decisions are made, who will be involved. Create that firm foundation so your disruptors can push off hard to reach audacious ambitions.

3. Insist on openness to create accountability and agency. Take advantage of the new normal of remote work and encourage people to share information and decisions in the open. If you can't physically see each other getting work done, then you need to tell each other what you are working on. Document every decision, even the most inconsequential ones, so that everyone knows everything. This will create accountability because, when everything is out in the open, there's nowhere to hide. When you have accountability, it also creates agency, where individuals step forward and take ownership of change and decisions. You will need every person to feel they are an integral part of the disruption strategy for you to succeed

4. Define minimally viable data for decisions. Time is your biggest enemy, because every day that you are not moving forward is another day that your future customer is moving away from you. Instead of collecting as much information as possible before making a decision, define what I call the *minimally viable data* needed to decide to move you forward just one step. As soon as you know that one option is a little better than the other, make the decision and try it out. Worst-case scenario: it doesn't work out and you can go back and try the other option.

5. Step out of your comfort zone. This is probably the hardest part about being a disruptive leader—you must keep yourself right at the edge of your comfort zone, because that is where growth happens. Over the past few months, we've all been thrown out of our comfort zone and come out the other end strong, more resilient, and determined to keep moving forward. The key is to find that edge where we are stretched—but not stressed. It takes courage to be vulnerable, to put yourself in a place of potential failure because it's the only way to move forward and grow. Model the path forward for your organization by stepping regularly and visibly out of your comfort zone so that others can follow your example.

Taking the first step with every step

I hope that you will leap high with courage and conviction so that you can be the disruptive leaders our world so desperately needs now. Anybody can be a leader because it doesn't require a title: a leader is simply someone who sees the opportunity for change and takes action to rally people to that cause.

I wish I could promise that the journey ahead will be smooth sailing. It's going to be anything but. That's what disruption is—it forces us out of our comfort zone and makes us come face-to-face with our biggest doubts and fears. But if you can look past them to the opportunities to serve created by disruption, you and your team will have a focus that will steady your hand.

All you can do today is to decide to take that first step on to the disruption path. And given the difficulties, every step will feel like the first step all over again. But trust and believe that you are on the journey, which will be so much better than staying mired in the past.

For the past two decades, **Charlene Li** has been helping people see the future. She's an expert on digital transformation, leadership, customer experience, and the future of work and the author of six books, including the *New York Times* best-seller *"Open Leadership"* and the co-author of the critically acclaimed book *Groundswell*. Her latest book is the best-seller *The Disruption Mindset*.

She's also an entrepreneur, the founder and senior fellow at Altimeter, a disruptive analyst firm that was acquired in 2015 by Prophet. Li was named one of the Top 50 Leadership Innovators by Inc, and one of the most creative people in business by Fast Company. She serves on the regional board of YPO, a global network of 28,000 CEOs. Li graduated *magna cum laude from* Harvard College and received her MBA from Harvard Business School. She lives in San Francisco.

EMPATHY IN HONG KONG

Martin Lindstrom

I admit it. I'm crazy. I went on a holiday to Hong Kong in mid-pandemic.

While everyone was disembarking the plane from Hong Kong, I boarded the return flight. I found myself in an almost completely empty plane, getting used to a new world where facial masks were obligatory. The immigration area was empty, the hotels were without guests, the streets were cleared of all signs of life.

Yet amid all that strangeness, I discovered lots of benefits. For instance, there were all those restaurants I'd never been able to get into. Like a dream, now they welcomed me with open arms. Hong Kong had turned into the bargain of a lifetime!

I know Hong Kong extremely well. During the past three decades, I've passed through this amazing city hundreds of times. I've come to know the people and the soul of the city, both before and after the Chinese takeover. Yet this time something was different. There had only been one casualty in this city of seven million, but the coronavirus had obviously taken its toll. The proximate cause? It boiled down to the facial mask.

Having worked extensively in Saudi Arabia, I had long thought about the impact of the obligatory abaya and headscarf worn by many women. I'd wondered how our ability to connect would be affected by being cut off from anything but another person's eyes. Now in Hong

Kong, I became reacquainted with a waiter I'd known for years. Behind his mask, all his familiar facial movements were invisible to me. When I asked him to remove his mask—staying outside the one-meter safe distance advised by doctors—I realized that the mask did much more than minimizing viruses. It also eliminated empathy.

Empathy is a topic close to my heart. I've studied it for nearly two years while writing my next book, *The Ministry of Common Sense*, due out in June this year. I know, at first empathy might sound like a fluffy topic. However, I've come to realize that empathy is the very backbone of humanity. We may not think about it every day, but even the tiniest facial movement, invisible to the naked eye but detectable by our subconscious mind, has been shown to have a profound impact on our ability to connect with other people. In fact, when mothers were asked to maintain a stone face in front of their baby, after only a few minutes the baby would launch into such a severe tantrum that it might last for hours. Studies even show that mothers who use Botox lose emotional connection with their children—all this, because of the loss of visual signs of empathy.

I realized it was that feeling I'd lost, as I walked the streets of Hong Kong. It was extremely unsettling. Losing the feeling of empathy was scary, to say the least.

According to a US study of more than 10,000 teens, the degree of empathy has dropped by a whopping 50 percent over the past decade. Accompanying this lack of empathy, we've also witnessed a spike in suicide rates; multiple studies confirm this surprising connection.

I'm writing this because the profound, unsettling feeling I had in Hong Kong is likely to define the future. The coronavirus will be long gone, along with its facial masks. There will probably be other global epidemics, but I'm not thinking about them. What I am thinking about is the loss of empathy caused by our change of lifestyle.

What happens when we're on our phones all the time, rarely looking up? What happens when our one-year-old's first step is recorded not by our eyes, but through the obligatory smartphone screen? What happens when we take six seconds to judge someone on Tinder, or when our fashionable earbuds are a fixed barrier as we scream to the world: *f . . . k off*? What happens when we only have 280 characters to express our true feelings on Twitter, or we polish our Facebook profile to such a degree that we aren't recognizable in it anymore, though it's perfect for the world to aspire to?

We lose empathy, that's what happens. We don't notice the loss, of course. It happens slowly, almost imperceptibly, just like placing a frog in a pot of cold water and turning up the temperature. Toss the frog in boiling water, and it would reflexively leap to safety—but turn up the temperature slowly, and the poor frog never realizes.

Empathy is what created the human species as we know it today. It's our imaginative ability to place ourselves in the enemy's shoes or predict what the bear will do, seconds before an attack. It's our ability to nurture and care for each other, rather than sliding into an online rage.

Yet that feeling of empathy, for which I once knew Hong Kong, seemed gone—replaced by fear and facial masks. And I began to sense a new virus spreading almost as fast as the coronavirus: the lack of empathy.

Martin Lindstrom is the founder of Lindstrom Company, the world's leading brand & culture transformation group, operating across five continents and more than 30 countries. *TIME Magazine* has named Lindstrom one of the "World's 100 Most Influential People". Lindstrom is among the world's top 20 business thinkers according to Thinkers50.

FIVE COMMITMENTS OF PURPOSEFUL LEADERSHIP

Jennifer McCollum

It was shaping up to be a very good year for our business, where we would reap benefits across the organization after nearly two years of investment in a significant transformation. Our strategic plan was working, and we had the people, products, and processes to thrive. On February 20, 2020, our head of operations walked into my office to alert me to a minor supply chain problem. We were having trouble getting some needed supplies out of China for imminent client deliveries. I chuckled, surprised that this so-called "China Coronavirus problem" was having an impact on our company. We quickly sourced a local supplier, and I assumed the problem had been solved.

Of course, that was only the beginning. As the news of COVID-19 escalated and fears grew globally, we each looked to our leaders for answers. At the macro level, we sought guidance from heads of state and health experts. Should we get on an airplane? Wear a mask? Make our own hand sanitizer? In our communities, we relied on local government to learn about the safety of our schools and gathering places. And in our organizations, we looked to the CEO and managers. Should we work from home? How do we respond to customers if services are disrupted or contractual terms need revising? Is *my* job at risk?

Even in the best of times, leadership is hard work; only 14 percent of over one million leaders in our Linkage database are rated by their managers, peers, or direct reports as *effective* when it comes to their impact on the people, culture, and business. However, we have identified a class of companies that consistently outperform expectations because they focus relentlessly on their leadership capability and capacity. Simply put, they prioritize their *people* in a way that has material impact on their business. These organizations can elevate the performance of their leaders and their workforce while building a great culture, even in dire times.

This has never been more relevant than it is today. In a crisis, when the path forward is unclear, leading is even harder. As CEO of Linkage, I am experiencing these challenges firsthand alongside leaders globally. And while none of us has all the answers, I do know one thing for sure: *every* one of us is doing our best to navigate this uncharted territory. Each day, I learn critical lessons and insights that help me connect with and communicate effectively with our employees, clients, partners, suppliers, and investors. It is times of crisis that have been the most important periods of growth in my career, accelerating my evolution as a leader.

In a crisis, ensure your purpose is your guiding light.

In fact, there is no more important time for each of us to reflect on our own sense of purpose. What is your calling? What is the unique value that you offer? What value does your team bring? What does your organization offer the world at a time when all our collective contributions are needed? I've found that grounding myself in answers to these questions has brought me important perspective in a time when it can be difficult to keep grounded in both our short- and long-term goals.

At Linkage, our purpose is clear: we exist to change the face of leadership, by accelerating all leaders to be more effective and by advancing women and other underrepresented populations. In challenging times, this mission becomes even more critical, as we help leaders operate more purposefully and inclusively, and emerge from this crisis even stronger.

It is in exactly this type of dynamic, uncertain environment that the most effective leaders stand apart from the rest. In fact, our research from more than 100,000 leadership assessments uncovered five common commitments that the most effective leaders make, which enables them to perform at higher levels and drive differential results.

Five Commitments of Purposeful Leadership®

1. Inspire. Leaders must provide hope and inspiration for the future, by directing energy toward a clear and bold vision. In a crisis, leaders still need to draw in others through their communication. Set shorter-term goals that can help rally and focus the team. Ask yourself: what can we accomplish this day, this week, or this month? And celebrate the successes, no matter how small.

2. Engage. This is a time to bring people together and ensure they have a chance to contribute to their fullest potential. With many decisions to be made and no road map to guide the way, inviting diverse perspectives will give you better outcomes. Open yourself up to others for their contributions.

We recently implemented a dynamic new process for cross-company collaboration, based on the Business Review Plan process I learned from Alan Mulally, former CEO of Boeing Commercial Airplanes and Ford Motor Company during the crises of 9/11 and the Great Recession. Every week, we convene eighteen leaders from every function and business unit to share information, identify immediate needs, and organize cross-functional teams to resolve them. Topics covered range from business continuity plans to employee communication and product innovation.

3. Innovate. Trying times demand accelerated change and reimagination of the business, given the realities of daily shifts in the external environment. To stay competitive and emerge stronger from a crisis, leaders need to drive new thinking.

COVID-19 is prompting massive innovation in health care, technology, education, and distribution. Suddenly, we are adjusting to a global remote workforce and school system. Scientists and regulatory agencies are collaborating at an unprecedented pace, testing new diagnostics, treatments, and vaccines. And demand for at-home delivery has outpaced supply, as evidenced by the lack of toilet paper on grocery store shelves. We are learning every day, focusing on what works, and staying agile.

4. Achieve. Successful leaders accomplish aspirational goals by creating appropriate clarity, structure, and process. In a crisis, loosening controls may be necessary, and a different structure may be required to allow rapid execution. For example, the Federal Drug Administration and other global regulators have lifted lengthy standard testing and approval processes, paving the way for faster solutions.

5. Become. Above all, in times of uncertainty, leaders must be emotionally present and resilient. We are called upon to put the good of the group ahead of ourselves. We need to be self-aware, courageous, and committed to being purposeful. It requires being calm and positive— standing strong in our plan, until we can develop an even better plan. It requires telling the truth and communicating openly about information and decisions as soon as we can. It requires resilience.

In addition to these commitments, our most recent Linkage research revealed another critical finding. Those who lead from a place of inclusion will quickly differentiate themselves, especially in a crisis where different perspectives and experiences are needed most.

We identified sixteen specific behaviors in our 360° assessments that map to inclusive leadership. For example, how well does the leader *"encourage a culture where people speak up, regardless of experience or background."* When we examined data from 19,000 assessments evaluating 1,200 leaders, we found that *the most effective leaders are also the most inclusive.*[1] In short, inclusive leaders will be instrumental in our ability to navigate a crisis and emerge from it successfully.

---

1. https://www.linkageinc.com/leadership-insights/linkages-latest-research -proves-the-most-effective-leaders-are-the-most-inclusive-leaders/

Upholding the commitments of Purposeful Leadership may require more of us than is reasonable during a crisis, and we can't do it alone. Ensure you have a support system with your peers or with a coach. Share your struggles, your hopes, and your fears, and ask for help. I benefit from weekly consultation from members of my personal Advisory Board.

One month into the crisis, the board, executive team, and I realized that the severe business impact of COVID-19 required us to lay off a portion of our staff so we could manage our cash. It is the most difficult decision a CEO must make, owing to the significant impact on culture and people. Using all the commitments of Purposeful Leadership, I dedicated myself and our leadership team to managing the difficult decision-making process with compassion and grace. We gathered the remaining staff to explain how our 2020 aspiration had been compromised, but outlined our plan to move forward, and invited them to ask questions and offer their perspectives and feelings. We thanked each departing employee individually and committed to helping them however we could in securing employment. I was moved by the emails I received from remaining staff, but even more moved from the public communication from departing staff, see examples below:

Head of Client Partnerships: "Yesterday was such a sad day. My head and heart ached for everyone at Linkage. You and the leadership team demonstrated such courageous leadership, with grace and humanity. Please know you are appreciated and inspiring. I am relentlessly committed to finding the opportunity in this massive disruption to help our firm innovate and thrive. We have incredible people and loyal clients, and together we will forge a path to a brighter tomorrow. Take care, and know that scaling to the summit remains the vision and my goal."

Project and Content Manager: "I wanted to thank you for the kindness you had during this terrible time. I know that the decisions made were not easy and that you are having a heartbreaking time as well. From last Tuesday until now I have felt Linkage's support. You all were so wonderful with giving the news and offering any help that was needed."

In the midst of crisis, may it be our collective goal to fulfill the commitments of Purposeful Leadership, and emerge stronger because of it.

Jennifer McCollum is CEO of Linkage, where she oversees the strategic direction and global operations of the Boston-based leadership development firm. For more than thirty years, Linkage has been changing the face of leadership. Through work with more than one million leaders, Linkage empowers leading organizations to develop effective, purposeful leaders; advance women leaders; and create cultures of inclusion. McCollum has twenty years of experience building and leading businesses in the leadership space. She has a master's degree in communications from the University of Stirling in Stirling, Scotland, and an undergraduate degree from Wake Forest University.

RAPID RESILIENCE DESIGN STRATEGIES

Rita Gunther McGrath

Bjarte Borjes is the chairman of the Beyond Budgeting Institute and the Senior Adviser for Performance Management at Norway's Equinor. He is one of the leading thinkers[1] on how we can create agile, responsive management practices that help organizations cope with what is often called the VUCA world, for Volatile, Uncertain, Complex, and Ambiguous. I've heard him use an analogy that to me is a wonderful point of departure for how we should all be thinking about strategies for leading that can respond deftly to crises such as that sparked by the coronavirus pandemic. With attribution, I'll borrow the analogy.

Consider a conventional traffic light. The rules of the traffic light are fairly blunt—stop, go, or slow down. The traffic light is not aware of its surroundings or even of what is going on right under its electronic nose. It doesn't know that at three in the morning, a driver patiently waiting for a green light could safely have driven through it, or that an accident has just happened, in which case everybody should get a red light. The rules governing traffic lights are typically preprogrammed using whatever data the traffic engineers had on hand at the time, but in most conventional systems the programs are fixed. Insidiously,

---

1. https://www.wiley.com/en-us/Implementing+Beyond+Budgeting%3A +Unlocking+the+Performance+Potential%2C+2nd+Edition-p-9781119152477

though, traffic lights create a false sense of clarity and rights of way, which can lead to accidents as drivers assume the system will keep them safe, or worse, try to game the safeguards in the system to accomplish their own purposes.

Consider, in contrast, a traffic circle. Or go beyond a traffic circle and think of an entire set of intersections and junctures devoted to the philosophy of "shared space,"[2] in which signals, signs, and curbs are removed. The signals of who has priority and who needs to give way were taken away. Drivers instead have to be alert and present. Without a guarantee of a right of way, they slow their speeds to a near-stop (increasing safety), while miraculously increasing the efficiency of movement through the intersection. Without the implied property rights of a green light, drivers need to accommodate one another to pass through, often signaling with hand gestures or other signals to other drivers, pedestrians, and bicyclists. With greater ambiguity about what each individual participant needed to do, everyone becomes more mindful.

'Make Everything as Simple as Possible, But No Simpler'

This phrase, attributed to Albert Einstein, cautions us against applying rigid, simple rules to complex, evolving situations. The traffic light has a limited repertoire of ways to influence the environment, designed in isolation from the situation at hand. The "shared space" environment on the other hand, elicits input from all involved participants in real time, adjusting the system even as individual participants seek to achieve their own purposes. So too, many leaders and executives have an oversimplified, rules-based approach to the resolution of organizational issues that squeezes out the potential genius of a more organic response. When we are dealing with an extraordinarily complex system, such as the coronavirus crisis, a different way of leading is indicated.

---

2. https://bigthink.com/want-less-car-accidents-get-rid-of-traffic-signals
-road-signs

Complex systems operate in ways that typically cannot be anticipated in advance, as opposed to systems that are just complicated. A complicated system—an aircraft, for instance—might well have millions of component parts, and yet for the most part these have been designed to work together in predictable ways. In contrast, the elements of a complex system interact in unpredictable ways. Each interaction can yield a different result. Thus, there are always unintended consequences. Further, the evolution of complex systems is path-dependent, meaning that earlier events can have a disproportionate effect, sometimes shifting the trajectory of the systems' development.

The challenges to human sensemaking capabilities when confronting complex situations are formidable. The presence of exponential effects, unintended consequences, rare events, limits to mathematical modeling, and irreversible effects are almost guaranteed to challenge the skills and intuition of even the most accomplished strategist. It is no surprise that so many leaders at this fraught time are simply scrambling to figure out what is going on.

Strategy designs for moving through a crisis

We are where we are. And that is right in the middle of the most significant inflection point that most of us will ever face in our lifetimes. Given what we know about how complex systems behave, here are five ideas for guiding your organization to discover its next steps.

1. Create the conditions for devolved responsibility. The old rules— our old traffic lights—aren't working and won't work in the changed reality we are facing. Think instead about how you might tear out the traffic lights and free your organization to act the way participants in a shared traffic space might act. Suggest some broad areas that you might consider to be important, and then promote the formation of small, cross-functional, even cross-organizational teams to consider how to plot your way. Say you were concerned about providing consistent customer support with a workforce based at home. Why not create the conditions under which small teams, working across the organization, can propose solutions and, perhaps, even have the authority to implement them? As former Gen. Stanley McChrystal observes, "if I'm making decisions someone else can make, it's a mistake."[3]

2. Generate lots and lots and lots of ideas and options from as many sources as possible. The reality of where we are right now is that there are no answers. Nobody can anticipate what will happen next in the complex system we have built. With this level of uncertainty, the best thing you can start to do is jump-start the learning in your organization by deploying what I would call discovery-driven thinking. Rather than conventional planning, in which your goal is to meet some kind of forecast and prove you were right, let's just admit that nobody is going to be right—what we want is to figure out what might be working and what might not be as fast as possible. So you want to create as many fast and inexpensive hypothesis tests about how your future will work as you can. Keep track of them, share the learning, and for now focus on generating lots of ideas—we'll get to convergence after the signals are more clear.

3. Create buffers in time. It is incredibly easy to become completely overwhelmed by the urgency of, well, everything that is going on and to try to cope with the deluge of demands on your and your people's time, patience, and emotional capacity. Just as doctors employ triage to figure out which patients they address first to maximize the number they can help, you need to do some triage on what you'll pay attention to right now. One discipline I can suggest is the "five most important" list. What are the five most important issues that you absolutely have to get right? The ones that, if you don't get right, the rest don't matter? Yes, those. Give yourself permission (with complete transparency with your team) to attend to the tasks that can be significant for those important five and put the rest in a queue. The goal is to chunk up the topics so that you can spend focused, purposeful time on them in sequence, not try to hold back the flood all at once.

---

3. https://mitsloan.mit.edu/ideas-made-to-matter/retired-us-general-stanley -mcchrystal-talks-leadership-strategy

4. Create buffers in space. Although it may seem counterintuitive, organizations with elements of redundancy can survive disruptions better than organizations that are excessively "lean." Here, give some thought to where you might create places in the organization that insulate its parts from interference by others. Redundancy, multiple paths, and substitutes are all useful. For example, if you are adopting a new way of working, and staff are widely cross-trained (creating redundancy), then if one operation is overloaded or cut off, others can step in to help. If there are multiple paths to a resource or an asset that people can use, having one out of commission is less problematic.

5. Define critical checkpoints and reevaluate your assumptions. With any discovery process, there is enormous value in pausing periodically, assessing what you have learned so far, and using those insights to take the next step. The military has a practice called an "after-action review," used to embed learning in its routine decision processes. The idea is to discuss what we hoped would happen, what happened, why we think it happened, and what this implies for the next set of decisions. It's incredibly important to make these discussions as psychologically safe[4] as possible, because you don't know if the idea that might save your organization will come from the people on the loading dock or the brand new hire.

Conclusion

We are at a historic moment, when many of the rules that we have taken for granted are about to be rewritten. The strategists' task is to help the organization make as much sense as it can, as quickly as it can, with respect to the path forward. With adversity, there is always opportunity. Try to keep that thought in mind, even as the rules are being rewritten around you. And remember, together you are more likely to get through that intersection safely.

---

4. https://hbr.org/podcast/2019/01/creating-psychological-safety-in-the
-workplace

Rita McGrath is a faculty member at Columbia Business School. She is an expert on strategy and innovation and is in the top ten of the Thinkers50 global management ranking. Her recent book is *Seeing Around Corners: How to Spot Inflection Points in Business Before They Happen*. For details, visit RitaMcGrath.com.

THREE STRATEGIES TO KEEP TEAM MEMBERS CALM AND PRODUCTIVE UNDER HEIGHTENED STRESS

Sharon Melnick

Too much to do, not enough time, constant change—pressure and exhaustion were already the norm. When crisis is overlaid, previous ways of living are forever disrupted.

Team members feel loss, and lost. Their emotions include panic, depression, or helplessness, which can interfere with effectiveness.

A Thrive Global study of 5,000 employees two weeks into the surge of the pandemic in the United States found that 85 percent of respondents experienced a lack of control and looked for help from their employer to manage their stress and uncertainty.

How your team members cope with a crisis will play a large part in determining the outcomes for your function or organization. As a leader, you can create the weather on the team.

Increasing team members' sense of control reduces stress and increases productivity. Your leadership can help them control three bases of their own successful coping: their Physiology, Psychology, and Problem Solving. Stress management is better defined as "self-management." Here are three strategies to maximize your team's sense of control in a crisis.

1. Physiology: Find the 'off switch' for anxiety and stress

Stress hijacks our nervous systems, but your leadership can be a counterbalancing force. Calm conditions come from coordinating between the two parts of the nervous system: the "On" (sympathetic nervous system, which gives focus and energy to solve problems and carry out work) and "Off" (parasympathetic nervous system, which gives access to calm and intuitive thinking).

'On' system. During a crisis, team members are in a state of heightened alert, hooked on the adrenaline of survival. Everything feels like an emergency and the ability to prioritize or delegate is compromised. Some may push themselves too hard and be unaware when they've passed their own limit of effectiveness or health.

The "On" state is highly useful for carrying out tasks, but can distort the thinking and feeling that fuel decision-making and focus: "On" system thinking can only reference the past to solve problems; there is an incapacity to think in new directions. Tunnel vision makes solutions shortsighted and expedient. Collecting information reactively leads to analysis paralysis. Survival-based filters prioritize "how does this affect ME?" perpetuating fear and overfocus on one's own issues.

'Off' system. In contrast, "Off system" thinking sees the big picture, accesses creativity, and thinks strategically for the long term. Our brains reason objectively, seeing the most meaningful options. We can access foresight and intuit what is "coming around the corner."

When it seems least possible to do, leaders must take a step back or build in time for this "Off" system, whole brain thinking. It's the "genius" button.

Balancing the "On" and "Off" systems creates a state of calm that maximizes problem solving and enables sustained focus. But how?

Create a schedule for yourself and the team with a "sprint-recovery" approach.[1] Schedule "On" system concentrated task time followed by a brief two- to three-minute rejuvenation break to access the "Off" system. Building in these brief periods of downtime or detachment may feel indulgent, but accessing the "Off" system in these recovery periods is key to maintaining your best performance.

Any moment that on- or off-the-job team members can access this calm or relaxation will help their mind optimize thinking and reset their body. It could be a good night's sleep, a short break to eat mindfully, or even thirty seconds to press the "Off button" walking down the hall. Here are some tactics to do that from my book *Success under Stress: Powerful Tools for Staying Calm, Confident, and Productive when the Pressure's On*.

Mental Reset breath. Mind follows breath, so breathing techniques are an easy recovery strategy. Try this Mental Reset strategy to balance the "On" and "Off" systems: inhale through your nose for five counts, hold for five counts, and exhale for five counts. Even two minutes clears your mind and yields calm relaxation and clarity. This brief mental vacation enables you to reevaluate priorities, access the best problem-solving parts of your brain, and have renewed energy to tackle challenges. It's best to do it midmorning, midafternoon, and before sleep. *(To make it easy to apply, I count out this breath for you at www.sharonmelnick.com/mentalreset.)*

By beginning team meetings with this two-minute Mental Reset, you can also help to recondition the nervous system of all members of your team (and get vastly improved meeting engagement).

Exhale breathing. If you only have a minute between tasks, breathe in to the count of four and out for the count of eight. Exhaling longer than you inhale activates the "Off" system, initiating a calm mind.

---

1. Tony Schwartz and Catherine McCarthy, "Manage Your Energy, Not Your Time," *Harvard Business Review*, October 2007, https://hbr.org/2007/10/manage-your-energy-not-your-time.

Mindfulness (intentional slowing of your breath and focused attention on the moment) is also a game-changer to continually access your "Off" system.

Sleep. An overactive "On" system is common in times of high stress, interfering with sleep. If you or your team members awaken in the middle of the night with worries, do left nostril breathing: cover your right nostril and breathe exclusively through the left nostril for three minutes. This activates the vagal nerve, chief nerve of the relaxation system.

Block time. Schedule time for "Off" system thinking into your calendar.

Presence. Your centered presence can help rewire your team members to find the calm of their "Off" system. Also, going through this crisis alongside them, you may face the human tendency to be "triggered." Start a daily self-check for signs of stress. Build self-awareness about your "re-actions," which can be "re-activations" of unresolved personal patterns. Have a clearly articulated "Horizon Point" of who you want to show up as in your leadership, which speeds recovery to centered state.

2. Psychology: Keep team members optimistic

Neuroscientists estimate humans have around 60,000 thoughts a day. How many of your team members' thoughts are constructive in an ever-evolving crisis?

Team members are playing mental movies in their minds, and when the future is unknown, and your leadership vision is ambiguous, they will fill in the blanks. The mental movies they play could be catastrophic. The antidote to fear is a clear path to an inspired future.

What's the best tone to motivate for an unknown future? Realistic optimism. *Optimism* paints a positive picture of the future you see, implying there's something each person can do to help achieve success. *Realism* sets the expectation that there will be discomfort and challenges, which can be adapted to and overcome. False reassurances will erode your credibility.

How can you find this tone in yourself to share with the team? Share information you're using as the basis for your optimism. Reflect on your own experiences, and how optimism has helped you be resilient to crisis situations. Tap any of your own guiding beliefs that help you maintain a sense of purpose and faith that crises are surmountable.

3. Problem Solving: Communicate to Find New Solutions

Your team members crave information. Honestly acknowledge problems, share rationales for decisions, and give updates on what you do and don't know. When others understand your logic, they more readily accept the outcomes and move forward.

They are overloaded. Memory becomes impaired in a crisis, so communicate in bite-size messages and repeat goals often.

They are fearful. Strong emotion will consume their attention and distract their focus. Actively reflecting their fears and frustrations, and genuinely holding space for their individual hardship can help break their loop of emotional spinning and improve their problem solving. Accept that their individual responses will vary across the full range of emotions.

They want to show their value. Actively seek to involve all your team members to stretch to the highest level of their ability. Though only some may proactively seek your attention, all of them are motivated (out of pride and self-preservation) to be involved in solutions. Cultivate a team-based Growth Mindset, which believes in the capability to learn new skills. It makes your team members ready to offer new ideas, and pivot to new duties. You could cultivate this opportunity seeking mindset with generative questions such as: How might this have happened "FOR" us, not "TO" us? Or What's the best idea we've ever shot down with "we can't" that could pivot to "what if . . ."

Find the leaders who will be 'born' in crisis. Give runway to the team members who step up in a crisis. Make them visible as part of cross-functional committees to find new solutions. Inspire them with the message "Now is your time!"

In short, your team members' lack of a sense of control will be heightened in a crisis and may significantly derail their ability to be productive or come up with innovative solutions for the path forward. As the leader, you create the weather on the team. How you manage yourself will strongly influence the team's outcomes.

You can encourage teams to think differently and sustain their focus by making space for "Off" time. You can motivate their Psychology with explicit messaging of Realistic Optimism. And your communication can help them optimize their Problem Solving toward new outcomes.

In a crisis, people often rise to the occasion—now it's up to you to help them do so.

Sharon Melnick, PhD, author of *Success under Stress: Powerful Tools for Staying Calm, Confident, and Productive When the Pressure's On*, is a leading authority on stress resilience and women's leadership. Informed by her research at Harvard Medical School, she speaks/trains at Fortune 500 companies and marquee conferences around the world, including the White House.

FIVE STEPS TO AVOID DISASTROUS DECISIONS

David Meltzer

During compressed times of uncertainty, we need to make decisions that help us seek our strength, health, and happiness. Create stability for ourselves and our businesses, then seek the opportunities that present themselves.

Uncertainty causes our ego-based emotions: Anxiety, Fear, Anger, Frustration, Inferiority, Superiority, and more. Ego edges goodness out of our lives and impairs our reactions.

To better understand how we tend to let uncertainty cloud our judgment, I talked with Dr. Gleb Tsipursky, CEO of Disaster Avoidance Experts, to discuss some of the most common decision-making mistakes that occur, especially in times of crisis. That conversation was so valuable that I have distilled it into five key steps to take to thrive.

1. Examine your values first

The best decisions we make are aligned with our values, so start by taking a daily inventory of your values. In times of stress or uncertainty, these values tend to shift, which makes it even more important to be consistent in this practice. I divide these values into four basic categories:

Personal values. These are the most valuable of your assets and include your integrity, character, honesty, discipline, work ethic, and love, among others.

Experiential values. This is where you invest your time and energy: your experiences, your situational knowledge, your education, all your successes, and the lessons you've learned.

Giving values. This comes down to the value you want to give to others. How can you be of service? Everybody is a gatekeeper of some sort. What value do you hold that you can share with others? Most importantly, can you give unconditionally, without the expectation of receiving?

Receiving values. Do you feel worthy of asking for what you want? Understand that money is a currency that must flow and that you are a vessel it can flow through. You also need to be able to shop for what makes you happy.

Most people would say our receiving values are most important. Whether the money is for you as a capitalist, leaving you as a victim, or flowing through you as a philanthropist, it depends on your perspective. Do you live in a world where there is more than enough for everyone? Do you feel like there is just enough? Or never enough?

Unfortunately, in times of stress, our values are constantly shifting. We can let our emotions get in the way of sound decision-making, which is why the next step is so important.

2. Take the long approach

For those who are older and more experienced, it is easier to take a long approach. They've lived through times of crisis before. For the younger generation, this can be a tougher perspective to hold.

You can still make decisions quickly, taking your values into consideration, but you need to be focused on the long term to avoid disaster.

- Use logic to filter whether your decisions are practical and pragmatic in the long run.
- Look at your long-term goals and ensure that every decision you make is aligned with those goals.
- Beware, as there are three reasons people tend to avoid taking this long approach:
  - People prefer not to think about long-term impacts.
  - People don't respond well to changing plans.
  - Many don't want to think about the fact the future might be different from the past.

Although it may seem counterintuitive, making decisions that consider long-term implications is more likely to get you where you want to be faster than if you make all your decisions focused on short-term gains.

3. Understand your cognitive biases

In a crisis, we tend to make decisions out of fear, often subconsciously. We can be reactive if we don't understand some of the underlying thought patterns that humans tend to follow.

Here are three examples Dr. Tsipursky says to watch out for:

Normalcy bias. We innately want to believe that things will function in the future as they have functioned in the past. This also means we are likely to underestimate both the likelihood of a disaster happening and its effects.

Planning fallacy. This relates to our ability to predict how much time something will take. We tend to be optimistic and underestimate the length of time something will take.

Hyperbolic discounting. Simply, people are more likely to choose a smaller reward if they get it sooner rather than waiting for the larger reward. THINK LONG TERM!

Your decision-making in trying times has to factor in these subconscious biases, or else you will be doomed to repeat them.

4. Contemplate a variety of scenarios, not a black or white view

Things are changing constantly, which is why you should be considering a wide range of opportunities that might occur. Combine the previous steps to examine what the future might hold for you and your business.

Accomplish this by working to frame things differently. To start, try to reinforce the long approach and think about what decisions you would make in the best-case scenario if time were not a factor.

Then, contemplate a more moderate scenario, focused on the more pragmatic details of your business—factor in things like time, cash reserves, and overhead.

Finally, taking a pessimistic approach is more to help you draw inspiration than to plan for your business. How would you react if something truly disastrous happens to your business or even you? Think about how much better off you are than any worst-case scenario and be thankful. When times are tough, maintaining that gratitude is essential.

Mentorship can also aid you. Human nature never changes, so seek advice from people who have lived through difficulties, whether they are the same experiences or not.

5. Be ready to make adjustments

Align yourself with your values. Align yourself with your team. Know that no matter what actions you take together, adjustment is essential.

Take the approach that whatever you are doing is a practice: mastery doesn't happen overnight, which is why we need to be prepared to adjust as we go. Use your situational knowledge to provide insight into which decisions will lead to profit, rather than disaster.

Know that no matter what scenarios occur, the unexpected will occur along the way. The more prepared you are by asking yourself tough questions and putting plans in place, the better position you and your business will occupy in the long run.

Don't manifest disaster

Nothing is more powerful when faced with a great challenge than a strong mindset. With these five steps and a deeper understanding of some of the most common ways that people mistakenly react to uncertainty, you will be empowered to make the right calls for your organization and yourself.

David Meltzer is the cofounder of Sports 1 Marketing and formerly served as CEO of the renowned Leigh Steinberg Sports & Entertainment agency. He is a three-time international best-selling author, a Top 100 Business Coach, the executive producer of Entrepreneur's number-one digital business show, *Elevator Pitch*, and host of the top Entrepreneur podcast, *The Playbook*. His newest book, *Game-Time Decision Making*, was a number-one new release. David has been recognized by *Variety Magazine* as their Sports Humanitarian of the Year and awarded the Ellis Island Medal of Honor

EXPONENTIAL LEADERSHIP IN CRISIS

Rob Nail

If ever there was a case to be made for "exponential leadership," it is in the face of a pandemic. The disruption that many business leaders face because of the exponential progress of some technologies is challenging enough. But when the exponential curve is that of a deadly virus like COVID-19, leaders must rise to the occasion to mitigate a truly existential risk. Becoming an "exponential leader" and knowing how to stay ahead of the exponential curve is critical for success and possibly survival through this crisis.

The Exponential Curve

The first and most critical mindset shift of the exponential leader is understanding the implications of exponential growth and recognizing that the change can be extremely deceptive and disruptive.

The disconnect between our linear expectations and exponential progress was best framed by Roy Amara and is known as Amara's Law: *"We tend to overestimate the effect of a technology in the short run and underestimate the effect in the long run."*

In the early part of the doubling pattern, an exponential curve is deceptive because it seems almost flat. For early-stage technologies, this typically results in disappointment as we underestimate how long it will take for the technology to come online. With a virus, it means that we will easily dismiss the most important signs when we still may have a chance to stop it. With a consistent exponential growth rate, by the time you can even see anything happen—say reaching 1 percent completion of a technology, or 1 percent of a population affected—we need only seven more doublings to reach 100 percent. In the case of COVID-19, we have seen infection rates doubling between every two and seven days, depending on region. Though an oversimplification, this means that without extreme efforts to slow this infection rates, once we hit 0.1 percent of a population infected, we have only twenty to seventy days before we would hit 100 percent infected.

Long term, we almost always radically underestimate how disruptive that exponential change will be.

Understanding the doubling patterns that are driving the pace of change (infection rates for virus or price, performance, capacity, and scale for technologies) and learning to forecast scenarios is critical if we are to more accurately anticipate the future. Too often, we rely on "experts" to project where technology will take us, but without an understanding of exponential growth, these experts are often wrong—really wrong—and with significant consequences.

Navigating exponential change

An accelerating pace of change and the widespread disruption it effects is nonintuitive and feels uncomfortable. Our brains have been hard-wired to think linearly for thousands of years. Learning to think and anticipate *exponentially* is incredibly hard—but critical.

At Singularity University, we developed a formula for helping individuals and organizations learn to embrace exponential thinking and adapt to this new paradigm by focusing on three areas: Mindset, Tools and Resources, and Network.

1. Mindset. An exponential mindset moves beyond incremental ideas and growth and explores big, bold, 10x, moonshot ideas to solve the most intractable problems. An exponential leader pursues something bigger than themselves and operates beyond the comfort of business as usual, pushing themselves and others to embrace change, overcome short-term hurdles, and vigorously pursue a better future.

2. Tools and resources. Many of the tried-and-true ways of building and managing a business are evolving. Core disciplines like strategy, leadership, and innovation must change to accommodate the new pace of change and persistent uncertainty about the future. Leaders must build new muscles, transform their cultures, and embrace new methodologies to ensure a resilient and adaptable organization prepared to ride each new wave of change.

Using frameworks such as Design for Exponentials, future forecasting, narrative-driven innovation (using science fiction storytelling), exponential leadership and organizations, and more, are ways that SU could help leaders envision a new future and develop solutions for the customers and problems of tomorrow.

The best way to fight an exponential virus is with exponential tools and technologies. Today, we have an extraordinary arsenal to deploy in the battle to identify, track, diagnose, treat, and mitigate a virus outbreak like COVID-19. An exponential leader needs to quickly learn how and when to use these tools and quickly deploy them all in an existential battle. Gaining access to critical population data sets from satellite systems or telecom traffic can quickly provide insights at the macro level. Partnering with the companies that provide the supercomputers that virtually everyone carries in their pocket today can provide diagnostic, monitoring, and initial treatment capabilities. Artificial intelligence, machine learning, hyperspectral imaging, gene sequencing, and CRISPR are just a few tools that every exponential leader should understand and possibly have in their tool chest.

3. Network
"When we try to pick out anything by itself, we find it hitched to everything else in the universe."—John Muir

It takes a collaborative and inclusive approach to tackle the most challenging problems. When facing a threat like a pandemic, the ability to communicate and share resources fluidly and with integrity is critical for survival. Valuing and being able to leverage partnerships on a global scale is a business amplifier and can also be a lifesaver.

Too little too late? In times of uncertainty and transition, when long-held beliefs are being reexamined, the natural human response is to hunker down and wait to move forward until it becomes apparent how things will shake out. If people do act before the new status quo is established, they do so slowly and after much analysis, using historical tools and outmoded assumptions. With a business facing technological disruption, this can mean an extraordinary missed opportunity or loss of value. When facing a virus, however, this slowness to act could mean the difference between life and death.

The exponential leader must be willing to stand up when it is most difficult and work to normalize what would otherwise seem against the norm.

As the first cases of coronavirus were identified in the US, many of my colleagues at Singularity University began discussing the quick action required to have any remote possibility of containment. While canceling travel for upcoming work trips is obvious in hindsight, there was significant pressure from event organizers and peers to not pull out of the meetings. Closer to home, we started wearing masks and gloves in public but found it to be awkward and looked at suspiciously even in the few days before the call to "shelter in place." Despite significant criticism and controversy, my wife and I decided to pull our kids out of school about a week before they closed anyway. We knew that these were the right things to do, but still second-guessed ourselves every step of the way in the face of others' judgment and perception.

This is the moment that the exponential leader is truly tested—having to face the stares and criticism for going against the status quo. In this case, we were a bit ahead of the curve and are healthy and safe, but upon reflection, we were far too slow to respond and put ourselves in unacceptably high-risk situations if the virus had a higher mortality rate.

Peter Diamandis, the cofounder of Singularity University, likes to say, "The day before something is a breakthrough, it is a crazy idea." For businesses, it is important to keep an open mind and use a principled approach to exploring those crazy ideas so that we don't dismiss them too soon. In the case of the viral threat, being viewed as "the crazy one" is a simple risk mitigation strategy—it is far better to be wrong and to have overreacted than it is to be right and not done enough.

Make no mistake: the global effects of COVID-19 will be staggering. However, the mortality rates of COVID-19 are not ultimately existential. Therefore, we should treat this as a test run, build our exponential leadership muscles, and be prepared to act swiftly when (not if) the next one hits us.

Rob Nail is global ambassador, associate founder, and former CEO of Singularity University. He is also a serial entrepreneur, engineer, adviser, investor, struggling author, and surfer, but mostly, a proud husband and father.

His mission is to build bridges for humanity to traverse technological disruption as quickly and gracefully as possible.

LEADING PROJECTS SUCCESSFULLY THROUGH A GLOBAL CRISIS

Antonio Nieto-Rodriguez

This is not the first time that the world has experienced a crisis. We had the terrible experience of 9/11 and the financial crisis in 2008 that swiped away millions of jobs in a matter of months. Yet we have never experienced something like the coronavirus. The speed of its spread and the severe impact that it has had across the world have been unprecedented, not only on the health of millions of individuals and on health care systems across the world, but also in its consequences to the global economy and society at large. Its full consequences remain unknown. The current situation is comparable, in small part, to the Second World War and the later recovery of a devastated world, through the Marshall Plan and other multibillion-dollar reconstruction initiatives.

Leadership is important in the tough and the good times, but even more important when a global crisis hits billions of people in a matter of weeks. It is especially important when leadership has lost much of its face value, as in the past few years, when we have seen the worst face of leadership in selfishness, hypocrisy, manipulation, etc.

I strongly believe we have an unparalleled opportunity to reinvent leadership. We can go back to the initial values and human beliefs of leadership, and improve them to address the current and future needs of our planet. The best way to do it is through **inspirational projects and strategic initiatives** to help organizations navigate through the crisis and transform to come up stronger.

From a practical and project leadership perspective, this is an opportunity for leaders to take action, step up, build the competencies, and move toward a more agile organization.

Leaders should focus and act upon three stages during this crisis. But even before that, leaders need to put on their "project" mindset: it is not about running the organization, it is about survival through projects. These are the critical steps:

1. Crisis management with agility

In normal circumstances, management will discuss an idea or potential project back and forth during several months before the project is approved, and resources and budgets are allocated—in addition to the administrative steps that need to be taking preparing a business case.

In a crisis, leaders ought to think fast and decide even faster. Most organizations will have a business continuity plan with the actions to trigger. Yet, the unpredicted magnitude of the coronavirus crisis requires leaders to be agile at adapting their contingency plans. They need to choose what the organization should do straight away to overcome, or at least mitigate, the impact of the crisis on their business and employees. It is likely that, given the magnitude of the crisis, some of the mitigating projects look like they won't succeed (e.g., launch of a promotion to keep customers buying services online), so leaders need to adjust course promptly.

In an unprecedented situation, where time is of the essence, the longer it takes for leaders to intervene, the more severe and costly the impact it will be. It is about making the right decisions—in a matter of days, sometimes hours—on problems and projects that in most cases had never been foreseen.

In late 2008, Fortis Bank, which had become one of the most prestigious banks in Europe after a joint acquisition of Dutch ABN AMRO a year earlier, came to the brink of collapse in a couple of weeks because of the financial crisis. The leadership of the bank was caught unprepared. To make things worse, the CEO left a few days into the crisis, leaving the bank without a captain and without leaders. Those left behind froze, and were not able to make decisions that would trigger rescue projects to overcome the deep crisis. No wonder the bank lost all its value in a matter of weeks and had to be bailed out by the Belgian government.

2. Stop projects ruthlessly, shift resources swiftly

At any given time, a large corporation will have hundreds if not thousands of projects on top of their day-to-day business activities; a small enterprise will have tens of projects running. Many are running at 100 percent capacity: employees and management are fully booked and there is no spare capacity,

The second stage is about freeing up capacity and resources as soon as possible. In normal circumstances, stopping projects can take a few weeks, if not months. But in a crisis, this phase should be carried out almost simultaneously as the first one. While leaders are selecting the mitigation projects, they have to decide which ongoing projects to cancel, which to put on hold, and which few projects should continue, in addition to the new ones being launched to overcome the crisis.

In my experience, in standard circumstances an organization can stop about 50 percent of their projects without any real impact on the business. However, in crisis mode, leaders should aim at stopping around 80 percent of their running initiatives.

This is something that requires not only agility, speed, and quick decision-making, but also some forward thinking. Teams need to know where the focus will be in the next weeks and months. If leaders struggle to decide, the whole organization will suffer.

3. Refocusing the organization

In the last stage, leaders need to decide where to focus the business once they overcome their crisis.

In addition to launching crisis mitigation projects, stopping projects, and freeing resources, leaders need to ensure that a smaller group of the organization is working on the near-term future. Let's not forget that there will be lots of new opportunities after the crisis.

It's essential that leaders focus on the immediate short term, but they should also think about those projects that will redesign and propel the business after the crisis, and start working on them. Often, it's about going back to what made the business successful, to its origins; sometimes it's about reinventing the business. This phase is as important as the previous two: it's an opportunity to reformulate your business strategy, your business model. Take advantage of that.

A great example is what Steve Jobs did when he returned to Apple in 1997. The company he had founded with Steve Wozniak was close to bankruptcy. Jobs decided that Apple had to return to its origins, to focus on its core capabilities. He canceled more than thirty products, refocusing on four (two laptops and two desktops), and he canceled about 80 percent of the projects, all those that were not linked to his vision and new Apply strategy. And he did all of this ruthlessly, shifting resources swiftly in less than a month.

This "Jobs approach" is what is expected from today's leaders to overcome the current global health and economic crisis.

These three phases will guide you through the crisis. If you act, make the tough decisions, communicate, shift resources, prioritize, and focus the organization, it is more likely that you and your team will get through the crisis. But you need to act immediately.

Antonio Nieto-Rodriguez is a leading expert in project management and strategy implementation, recognized by Thinkers50 with the prestigious award Ideas into Practice. He is the author of *Lead Successful Projects* (2019, Penguin), *The Project Revolution* (2019, LID), and *The Focused Organization* (2012 Gower). He has been teaching project management for more than a decade to senior executives at Duke CE, Skolkovo, Solvay Business School, and Vlerick. Nieto-Rodriguez has held executive positions at PricewaterhouseCoopers, BNP Paribas, and GlaxoSmithKline. A former chairman of the Project Management Institute, he is the cofounder of the Strategy Implementation Institute and the global movement Brightline. He is a member of the Marshall Goldsmith 100 coaches.

HOW TO USE STRATEGIC BEGINNER'S MIND IN TIMES OF UNCERTAINTY AND CRISIS

Richie Norton

I received an unexpected request for a meeting from Stephen M.R. Covey, former CEO of FranklinCovey and author of the best-selling book *The Speed of Trust*. In his conference room, Covey told me that, after hearing me speak at a recent event, he hoped I might consider coming to work for him presenting *Speed of Trust* training.

As soon as I scooped my jaw off the floor, I told him that, although I was flattered, I felt I was too young and inexperienced even to entertain the idea. I asked, "What would the gray hairs think?"

Then, Covey taught me a priceless principle that would forever change my outlook on the nature of education and experience.

He said, "Richie, experience is overrated. Some people say they have twenty years' experience, when, in reality, they only have one year's experience, repeated twenty times."

That statement blew my mind and opened windows of opportunity all around me. In an instant, I felt free from the self-inflicted mental bondage I had created for myself about my age and my feelings of experience-based inadequacy. I suddenly realized that if something was important enough to me, if I was truly committed to achieving success, I could learn what I needed to know along the way! In an instant, one statement that I had never considered before had changed my mind from fearing a great opportunity with negative thinking to embracing a great opportunity with optimism and enthusiasm.

Get better, not bitter: The strategic beginner's mind

Successful people continuously learn new things and implement them. One challenge that seasoned leaders face in times of crisis and red-alert uncertainty is that they fall back on experiences that don't fit the times—*stale leadership.* While the tried-and-true has worked in the past, it's confusing when an out-of-scope disruption puts everything you thought you knew out of focus.

Don't get bitter; get better.

Stale leadership is like trying to complete a multidimensional jigsaw puzzle with flat, tabletop puzzle pieces from a different set. To stay relevant and effective amid change, leaders must embrace what I call the "strategic beginner's mind." *Shoshin* (初心) from Zen Buddhism means "beginner's mind." The concept is to rid yourself of preconceptions when studying something as if you were a beginner.

As Marshall Goldsmith put it, "What got you here, won't get you there." A strategic beginner's mindset combines your seasoned experience to *unlearn* and *learn* rapidly to solve problems with creativity in times of complexity.

Leaders who deploy a strategic beginner's mindset find themselves making decisions at the crossroads of 1) what worked in the past and 2) what will work now. This critical time between *what used to work* versus *what will work now* is a powerful opportunity that few leaders tap into with grace.

. . . but you can.

If you effectively apply these strategic beginner's mind principles in crisis, you will create and use tactics that achieve desired results with less risk and increase trust with your stakeholders. Here is a framework to get better, not bitter in a crisis. Use these three "asks" to learn rapidly, implement effectively, and become a better leader under time pressure, crisis, and change.

1. Ask stakeholders to embrace a strategic beginner's mindset. Here's a fast, eight-point directive or checklist to implement in your organization as you practice a strategic beginner's mindset in times of uncertainty:

1. Execute for results using real-time information for real-time success.
2. Identify and unlearn the "best practices" that aren't working.
3. End the circumstantially bad "best practices" in all corners of your organization where needed, effective immediately.
4. Actively signal to your organization in word and deed directly (from the front line to the C-suite to the board and all stakeholders) to remember that leadership is a choice, not a title (so they can better lead in their own sphere of influence).
5. Ask middle management to be an unusually helpful facilitator of information flow—even if that means the frontlines and executives speak directly.
6. Activate helpers to do the job without fear of potential negative consequences, because doing nothing or retreating would be worse.
7. Tell your people you have their back.
8. Repeat.

By following each of the eight points, you will learn more about your organization faster than you may have before. It may scare you what you learn. That's okay.

All people get caught on their heels, flat-footed, or tiptoeing—but successful people take a knee. Take a moment between thought and action to pause and reflect. Then, take 100 percent responsibility for the success or failure as if it all depends on you . . . and trust your people to go to work. *Warning:* you may have to drop being defensive of old patterns and even policies that don't serve your stakeholders anymore.

2. Ask better questions, get better answers. I do a lot of work in China. I'm the CEO of a strategic product development and end-to-end supply chain company, and we work globally every day. In January 2020, our suppliers in China told me about what they were seeing, experiencing, and hearing in China concerning what we now know as COVID-19. In a turn of events, they asked us to help get them supplies they would normally supply us with for our work.

We immediately asked questions. How can we help? Who can help us? Where is the immediate need? Where will the need be next? We decided to see who was not being helped and to help there. This led to us sharing with our clients around the globe what we thought might be coming, based on what we were learning in China (despite politics and news media mania).

We then went through the scenarios of what would happen, we predicted the supply chain issues the best we could, and we formulated a plan. We informed our stakeholders and brought them into our strategy sessions.

In doing so, our stakeholders are better, not bitter. In times of crisis, if you choose not to serve your customers, they will find someone else or something else to meet their needs. Don't become irrelevant. Get creative.

I received a lot of resistance and for sounding the alarm long before COVID-19 directly affected my country and our businesses. Resistance in times of crisis is a small price to pay to achieve resilience. We asked the naysayers better questions and we were able to come up with better answers to unite others to a common cause. Creative leadership prevailed as we used a strategic beginner's mind to "start over." Through inventiveness and resourcefulness, we created new, valuable opportunities to meet the needs of our people up and down the supply chain.

Starting with a better question takes you down a better path. Instead of asking, "What do I need to do next?" Ask yourself, "Who do I want to be?" You'll know what to do when you know who to be. What question haven't you asked yourself? You're only one question away from a life-changing, timesaving, innovative answer.

3. Ask for the new normal to be embraced fully. In crisis, you and your people may be experiencing trauma and grief. Recognize those feelings in yourself and others. As has been said, "name it to tame it." Your feelings aren't necessarily indicators of where to go next, but rather a gut check to get centered.

When my son died from a communicable disease (pertussis), I learned that grief is debilitating. Your people are feeling the pains of losing their identity, losing the way things were, having challenges at home on top of major losses. Your people may feel debilitated. Recognize individual pain out loud by saying "I'm sorry."

I've learned that grief is a tunnel, not a cave. You as a leader must take them toward the light without diminishing how they feel. Help people embrace the "new normal" in an empathic way.

The new normal doesn't mean that things won't get better, but it does mean that things aren't going back to the way things were. Today, with COVID-19 and future crisis, it is essential to embrace the new normal—lead with a blend of realism and optimism into the unknown leveraging a strategic beginner's mind.

When you fully embrace uncertainty, you can fully engage in the way you want things to be. The opposite of certainty in life is called freedom. If you want to be free, you must be willing to advance your leadership into the uncertain.

Drop the "act" that you know what you're doing, and you'll know what to do. Use a strategic beginner's mindset to win the battle. Fairweather idealists inherently can't survive storms. Battle-ready idealists can survive anything. Be battle-ready. Use your strategic beginner's mind.

Richie Norton is the best-selling author of *The Power of Starting Something Stupid*, CEO of Global Consulting Circle, and cofounder of PROUDUCT—idea-to-market innovations. He received his MBA from Thunderbird School of Global Management. Richie is married, has four boys, and lives on the North Shore of Oahu, Hawaii.

FINDING OUR FINEST HOUR

Laura Gassner Otting

Crisis brings out the worst in people. But it also brings out the best in people. What if it brought out the best in you, your team, your company?

What if you could get to the other side of this crisis knowing that in the greatest hour of need of those who rely upon you, you did in fact have, as Churchill called it, your "finest hour"?

You can. And the answer is simple: be of service, be you, be better.

The first part of the equation—*be of service*—demands that we finally reconcile that we can hold both altruism and strategy in our hands at one time. We've often been told that one comes at the price of the other, but this crisis will show us that each cannot just peacefully coexist, but augment the other.

In an environment where current money is scarce, where deals are not being inked, where bleeding is being stemmed and cuts are more prevalent than growth, there is no need to focus on maximizing today's revenue. The revenue that is there, or proximate, is what there is. Land grabs won't yield much more than frustrated energy, and leaders pursuing this path will look selfish at best.

On the other hand, opportunities to be of service are plentiful.

Think about your business. What can you do for others, today, this week, this month, for free or low cost? If your work, like mine, is dead in the water, you aren't making any money now anyway. And, you are panicking on a daily—hourly?—basis. So, what can you offer to others that provides value, gives them some help, demonstrates your brilliance? You can always charge later, but successful leaders will use this time to be of service. It will help your heart, it will show your character, it will bond you to your employees and customers in true and authentic ways. And, they'll remember it tenfold in the future when money is flowing again.

In other words, future money is worth more than current money.

The second piece of the equation is to *be you*.

Leaders are often asked to be perfect. We are told that we must always know what to do, what to say, how to act, how to react. This new world didn't come with a user's manual, and there is no way to get it perfectly right. Being you is the only thing that you know how to do: leaders who show humanity, even if it lacks grace or poise or confidence at times, will win the day.

So, how do you be you? Drop the figurative (and literal) green screen.

For fifteen years, I sold executive search. I sold an impeccable read of talent honed through years of Jewish mothering and witchblood genetic evolution. I sold a deep and wide research function the likes of which the CIA would envy. I sold a teeming database, a "little black book" that would make the Fonz chew his fist.

But, most of all, what I really sold was trust.

Every search firm that lined up in the waiting room walked in to pitch the search committee and gave, in some form or another, the same presentation: we're smart, we're deep, we're fast, we're, at the very least, equal to the value proposed in our price. And it was all true. We operated among the elite, the best and the brightest, the most qualified to do this work in the exceptional ways our clients deserved and demanded.

In the end, it came down to one thing more than anything else: who did the client trust?

We are all in crisis. We are all stressed. We are all on quarantined sands that seem unrecognizable one day to the next.

Yet, there is also a rush to appear like we've got it all together, like we are perfect. We are green screening away our personalities and trying to look as if we are unaffected by this axis-tilting event. Frankly, this approach helps no one.

I'd like to see your bookshelf. I'd like to see your 5K medals. I'd like to see your family pictures. I'd like to see your art. I'd like to see your puppy. I'd like to see your backyard view. I'd like to see your neglected pile of laundry (because then I'll feel better about mine).

I'd like to see *you*.

Extroverts need the connection and the ability to root around in your life. Introverts (like me) need the voyeuristic opportunity for conversation starters, the discovery of which are so otherwise exhausting to purchase. Humans, of all stripes, need to be human. Your efforts to hide that through polished perfect green-screened lives are no better than carefully curated social media posts of a life or business personality that isn't real.

Your efforts to hide who you are leave your isolated team lonelier than before, for the effort placed to keep our connection at bay is even more obvious and intentional now. It's not that I realize I don't know you. It's that I realize you never wanted me to in the first place.

The final piece of the equation is to *be better.*

No, that's not meant in some rise-to-the-equation successories-type meme. It means that you will assuredly get better at one thing during this crisis, and that's change. Change is stressful, change is scary, change is often avoided at all costs even though leaders are brought in with the specific mandate to enact just that.

Here's a silver lining of COVID-19: we all are going to have to get comfortable at being uncomfortable. And that's going to make everyone better: better at change.

This crisis is a war, not a battle. And, as in any war, the key to completion is getting deep into the cave of suffering and making friends with its hobgoblins. Play the long game, practice grace, know that everyone gets to the finish line at their own time, in their own finest hour. And, when they do, they'll have crossed the Rubicon and realized that change didn't kill them, but made them stronger.

Together, apart, we will lead one another through this.

Laura Gassner Otting is an author, speaker, and executive coach. She is the *Washington Post* best-selling author of *Limitless: How to Ignore Everybody, Carve Your Own Path, and Live Your Best Life*, a member of the MG 100, and was recently voted as the #2 Startup Coach and #10 Motivational Speaker of 2020 by Global Gurus International.

ORGANIZATIONAL LEADERSHIP THROUGH THE PANDEMIC

Rafael Pastor

As a board member of several companies and not-for-profits, I have admiringly observed (and occasionally assisted) their CEOs and executive teams cope with and battle a pandemic that created immediate and complex emergencies that none had experienced before. Each of these CEOs and their teams has risen to the challenges with courage, compassion, and take-charge effectiveness. Although the organizations are different in size, sector, and culture, all their leaders have acted by implementing these five imperatives:

1. Protect and preserve

First, leaders must protect their people—their employees, customers, and other stakeholders. This has required not only following governmental directives for safety, health, and epidemic mitigation. Frequently, the organizational leaders have acted *ahead* of government officials—shutting down operations, requiring employees to work remotely, providing vital information to their communities.

Simultaneously, leaders must preserve their organizational assets—capital (cash), reputation (brand), and resiliency (survival). This has required drawing down debt facilities to maximize cash reserves;

cutting back on or deferring payroll, rent, capex, and other expenditures; and maintaining only essential ongoing operations. These are difficult—even painful—actions. They must be done surgically, transparently, and consistently with the organization's mission and values. Most heart-wrenching are the decisions to lay off or furlough employees where necessary for the ultimate survival of the organization. In some cases, the choice is between immediately depriving valued employees of a paycheck and saving the company so the employees can later return to their jobs.

2. Communicate and console

Uncertainty and fear are themselves a pandemic. Just as the COVID-19 virus requires widespread behavioral and ultimately immunological antidotes, uncertainty and fear require clear communications and compassionate consolation—which organizational leaders must provide repeatedly. All stakeholders (sometimes collectively, sometimes separately) must be forthrightly informed in real time of the what, why, and how of the decisions being made by the leaders—and, over time, what decisions were changed. Fortunately, technology has enabled these communications to be instant and targeted. But they must also be genuinely caring, focused on alleviating as much as possible the doubts and apprehensions of the recipients. Leaders who had the prepandemic trust of their communities can tap into that reservoir of goodwill much more readily than those that didn't. Credibility is essential.

3. Adapt and adjust

The pandemic's impact and trajectory change by the day, sometimes by the hour. It's critical for leaders to stay thoroughly informed, to be nimbly adaptive, and to adjust how they are reacting to changed circumstances. This includes further downsizing operations and personnel, developing contingency plans, and calculating the short- and long-term impacts on the financial and even existential viability of the organization. An important challenge has been to understand and take advantage of federal, state, and local emergency economic assistance programs, including loans to large corporations, SBA loans to small businesses, and expanded unemployment benefits. This can require seeking legal advice, joining lobbying efforts, and updating financial forecasts and models. Leaders must identify what they don't know and seek guidance from their counterparts at similar organizations, their board members, and outside advisers.

4. Project and plan

Hard as it may be to see the light at the end of the tunnel, leaders must try to foresee the road beyond the tunnel. Alternative projections (best, middle, and worst cases) and time frames (short, medium, and long terms) must be devised for the organization. And alternative recovery plans must be designed accordingly. The fundamentals of business plans need to be applied, almost as for a start-up: assumptions and calculations about available funds, potential revenues, rehired personnel levels, operating and capital expenditures, debt capacity, etc.

Even more difficult to forecast—but necessary for the assumptions—are the postpandemic structural and societal "overhang" changes that will affect the organization. How soon will unemployment levels decline? Will more people continue to stay at home and work remotely? Will people rush to restaurants, movie theaters, retails stores, and travel because of pent-up demand, or will they be reluctant to do so because of both continued fear and diminished personal funds? Will enhanced, new opportunities for growth and value-creation develop for certain sectors (e.g., financial services, insurance, technology, life sciences, pharmaceuticals, etc.)? As hard as such scenarios are to predict, they must be factored into the projections and plans being formulated amid the crisis.

5. Perspective and positivity

Finally and perhaps overarchingly, leaders must have a historical perspective and a positive outlook in their decisions, communications, and conduct. This does not mean they should shirk recognizing dire circumstances, nor should they have a Polyanna-ish attitude. But it does mean they should demonstrate and inspire the confidence that "we'll get through this." This entails reminding their communities of some things: that this country has been through and overcome even greater crises; that we all have faced and survived personal hardships; and that the organization itself will be adaptive and resilient based on everyone's strength and support. The key to the effectiveness of such messages is for the leaders to have an unflinching belief in themselves, their people, and their organization. If they say (literally or effectively) "we have nothing to fear but fear itself," they must themselves be authentically fearless.

Rafael Pastor has an extensive and diversified track record in running successful businesses and advising business leaders. His career as an attorney, investment banker, and CEO has spanned the media/entertainment, education, and business/financial services sectors. He now serves on a variety of boards and as an adviser.

From 2004 to 2013, Pastor was chairman and CEO of Vistage International, the world's largest for-profit CEO membership company (which he co-owned with Larry Ellison, Michael Milken, and Thomson Reuters).

CRISIS LEADERSHIP: RECOGNIZING AND MAXIMIZING CRITICAL JUNCTURES

Beth Polish

When a company faces a crisis, people often say it's at a critical juncture. But a crisis and a critical juncture are not the same. Broadly defined, a crisis is urgent, un-ignorable, often sudden, and potentially dangerous or fatal. A critical juncture is a choice to go down a particular path with far-reaching implications that often can't be undone, and are not always easy to see.

In times of crisis, with survival decisions being made every day, using the terms interchangeably can mean solving the crisis at the expense of recognizing the pivotal critical juncture that the crisis and its resolution have created—meeting the short-term demands of the crisis but missing the crucial need for long-term reinvention.

Whether it's a country, a company, or a person, every crisis creates change. The ecosystem morphs and adapts, and you can't control all the changes. At the heart of great crisis leadership is embracing the understanding that you have to solve for both—the crisis itself and the critical juncture you'll face coming out of it into a changed world.

What's in a name?

In the business world we spend a lot of time thinking about titles. Director, managing director, vp, associate, manager. Titles define who you are and how people perceive your role. How does someone get one of those titles? By working hard? Delivering results? Sometimes. But to a lot of people the way to get a better title is by knowing how to navigate corporate politics. We see the same thing in the public sector, except there the labels are clearer. We call the people we elect to represent us "politicians." We don't call them "leaders." While they say they're going to represent everyone, no one expects it. Because they're always looking to their next election—a.k.a. keeping their job—everyone assumes that politicians are only interested in the people they think will keep them in office.

Real leaders in a time of crisis are working for everybody they're leading, not just the people who put them in power, or who can protect their job, or get them reelected. They have to let go of what led them to succeed in favor of doing what's truly needed.

Great leaders know that a crisis will change the world. They understand that nothing else matters if they're not open to the relationship between the crisis and the critical juncture it creates. The crisis-born critical juncture may give them the opportunity they've been looking for to go down a particular path, or it may force them to abandon it and find a different path. Either way, the doorway to a new world is open.

Slow down to speed up

Growing up, I was a horseback rider. I loved spending my summers at a riding school in rural Vermont learning the ins and outs of combined training—the sport where horse and rider compete in dressage, cross-country jumping, and stadium jumping. I think I loved it so much because each phase demanded different thinking and skills, all from the same horse and rider.

The first thing a rider needs to do is walk the course to decide what pace for each section is right so she can finish on time and without penalties. You have to make a plan, knowing that you can't control for everything. The course will change as the competition progresses. You have to observe how the other competitors are doing, pay attention to the jumps you're particularly concerned about. Be ready to adjust your plan along the way, based on what you've learned and on what you see as you take the jumps yourself.

To propel themselves over those fences, horses need to have their weight on their hind legs. Yet, to make time, the horse-and-rider team often has to gallop between fences, which puts the horse on their front legs. If they don't find a way to switch gears and get on their haunches, they'll end up going right through the fence.

So about three or strides out from the fence, the rider will "sit down" on the horse (riding at a gallop puts you up off the saddle like a jockey). In response to this signal, the horse will slow and lean back on its hind legs to give it the power and position to propel itself—and its rider— up and over the fence. It's a delicate balance between getting that energy to go up and maintaining the momentum of the gallop so the team goes up and forward and doesn't crash through the fence or come down on top of it. Horse and rider literally slow down to speed up (and over).

Successfully getting through a crisis and navigating the associated critical junctures takes a comprehensive plan and the nimbleness to adjust it in midstride, plus the same sort of toggling between two different types of energy and dynamics it takes to clear a jump. The need to meet the crisis aggressively has to coexist with the thoughtfulness needed to make the right choice at the critical juncture. Great leaders find a way to slow down enough to successfully read the course and the world, and then lead their company along the right path out of the critical juncture—and not gallop headlong through it.

Are you hearing me?

Some people have great success getting people to adopt their point of view, or at least listen to and consider it. Most people don't.

The crisis we're in now has shown us at least one great example of what works. Drs. Deborah Birx and Anthony Fauci, globally recognized experts in public health, infectious diseases, and epidemiology, were asked to join the White House Task Force on the COVID-19 pandemic to educate people who had no experience dealing with a medical crisis like the coronavirus.

They weren't the first to try to get the White House to understand the magnitude of the global COVID-19 pandemic. But they were the few who have had real impact. Why were they able to succeed where others failed? CNN reported on April 2 that Birx and Fauci saw that the president responds to charts rather than prose. So they produced charts that showed the numbers, bringing their projections to life. And they made those charts large, so there was no ambiguity in the story they told.

They knew the secret of getting their message across: That the person trying to communicate has the responsibility to find a way that's effective with the people they're talking to. That if they want to be heard, it's on them to adapt. It's not up to the person being communicated with to change the way they hear.

Crises make people afraid. Telling it straight can take away some of the fear, but only if the people hearing it can understand.

Drs. Birx and Fauci were at a critical juncture: they had one chance to convince their audience. They could have given a formal lecture, but instead they took charge by meeting their audience where and how it could hear best. That's leadership.

Winston Churchill and the power of a leader's language

"In these dark days the Prime Minister would be grateful if all his colleagues . . . would maintain a high morale in their circles; not minimising the gravity of events, but showing confidence in our ability and inflexible resolve to continue the war till we have broken the will of the enemy . . ."

Churchill followed his own advice. He led by example, never minimizing the seriousness of what the British people were going through and always showing the confidence and resolve he asked of others. He got out to the factories and the bombed-out neighborhoods, so the country he was leading could see his conviction firsthand. He inspired people to be resilient through the tough, terrifying months of the Blitz and at the same time to look toward a future they could build together. Like countries, companies face crises both large and small. And when the crisis is global (whether it's a fundamental change in an industry or a worldwide pandemic), it's that much more urgent for everyone.

But it's in the critical junctures that come out of a major crisis that we can clearly see great leaders in action. They accept that their business (or their city, or country) won't go back to the way it was. They're energized by what's possible ahead; at the same time, they're focused on tackling the immediate crisis. They communicate the challenges that need to be faced and, like Churchill, they give the people they're leading a sense of having control over their own destiny, a vision for the future, and the opportunity to rise above what they ever thought possible. And just as Churchill knew that his words resonated far beyond his shores, to Washington and even to Berlin, great corporate leaders know they are talking not just to their team but beyond them to all employees, and to customers, partners, even competitors.

Churchill himself got to the heart of it. Told that the best thing he had done during the Blitz was to give people courage, Churchill disagreed. "I never gave them courage," he said. "I was able to focus theirs."

All along the way, a leader faces critical junctures—the first being to decide what kind of leader to be, and the last, and most important, to determine their exit strategy coming out of the crisis. If you chart the crisis for its critical junctures and make the right choices, your company will come out on a new path in a changed world, and you will come out a different person as a leader.

Beth Polish, founder of the Critical Junctures Group, LLC, helps companies and leaders identify and successfully navigate critical junctures. A pioneer in the NYC digital community, she was founding COO of iVillage, cofounder of Dreamlife with Tony Robbins, and Head of Corporate Innovation at Hearst. Polish has an MBA from Harvard and a BS in Anthropology.

TRANSFORMATIONAL GROWTH AND DISRUPTIVE CHANGE

Mark Thompson

*(Note: this article originally appeared in AMA Quarterly,
Winter 2017–18.)*

In 2017, more than five historic hurricanes ripped across thousands of
miles of the Northern Hemisphere, setting new records for destruc-
tion. Millions of people were plunged into darkness. In the wake of
these storms, whole communities struggled to rebuild both their personal lives and their businesses.

In some respects, we are all experiencing a version of this drama
and trauma at the office every day, aren't we? Do you know anyone who
is not battling a series of sudden superstorms erupting in their industry or business? Is there anyone out there enjoying business as usual?
The macroeconomic environment is serving up breathtaking disruptions with greater speed and such ferocious frequency that yesterday's
superstar leaders and global brands are quickly outpaced or overcome
by more effective competitors. We're all feeling the overwhelming pressure of change at work, whether we signed up for it or not.

Even one of the most powerful entrepreneurs in the world isn't safe
from disasters in nature and business.

As Hurricane Irma tore through his family home on Necker Island in the British Virgin Islands, Virgin Group's Sir Richard Branson and the remaining staff members on the island shivered in the basement. Deafening winds pummeled the walls like live ammunition, blowing out windows and doors and tossing buses and cottages like toys in *The Wizard of Oz*.

This was not the first time disaster had struck his home.

Just three years earlier, a single bolt of lightning incinerated his house. Now he was again taking refuge as yet another storm raged outside his newly rebuilt home in that same location. And like most of his neighbors in the BVI and elsewhere in the Caribbean, Sir Richard would be starting over, again.

"If you're complacent, resting on your laurels, thinking you're somehow safe and above it all, disruption will come and get you!" Sir Richard says. "But this isn't about blaming others, becoming mired in victimhood, or surrendering to difficult circumstances."

Embracing growth in a chaotic environment takes resilience and persistence, and you can't take the risk of standing still or ignoring what's changing around you. As a leader in your own life and work, "you have to be the change you wish to see," Sir Richard says, paraphrasing Gandhi. "You can't scale up a company faster than you're willing to scale your own personal and professional growth."

You can't transform your organization any faster than you're willing to change yourself, Sir Richard believes. In a wild time where you're expected to grow your business faster every quarter, "your job is to build a new you and engage a new us who's better at what you do."

Leaders struggle to define success

In a global survey we conducted in 110 nations, we asked high achievers about their definition of success in this new world. Even the most accomplished leaders are feeling under siege to accommodate what seems like contradictory pressures to accelerate growth while lowering costs. They're struggling to balance the dynamic needs of four generations of employees, clients, and stakeholders who themselves are now in a state of perpetual and unpredictable change driven by disruptive competitors, new technology, and shifting market demands.

Best-selling author Brian Tracy and I wrote a business leadership primer about how to manage in chaotic times in our book, *Now, Build a Great Business!: 7 Ways to Maximize Your Profits in Any Market* (AMACOM, 2010).

The trends we've seen in our research have become obvious in our coaching practice too. The greatest challenge for leaders today is activating their own willingness to continue to role-model change by demonstrating growth as individuals, and then engaging their people to drive change rather than be run over by it. Those who cling to the status quo, or who resort to defending past successes with complacency or denial, do so at their own risk.

We discovered in our research that high achievers don't have just one definition of success. We found three distinctly different ideals that collide as drivers of their behavior: Purpose—Performance—Passion. You will often hear these words being tossed around as synonymous, but our World Success Survey revealed they are distinctively different but related concepts.

Purpose means that you're pursuing a mission or ideal that's larger than you as an individual; it could be a company, community, or other organizational ideal. Some people think of this as their legacy. **Performance** means that you're driven to produce results and have impact for that Purpose—it's something you care enough about to collaborate and even compete with others to win. In this context, **Passion** is about what drives your heart more than your head. It's what you'd secretly do for free because it intrinsically motivates you. You care about many other things in life and work, but those things that ring the triad of these definitions of success simultaneously—Purpose, Performance, Passion—create the formula for sustainable success.

The No. 1 priority for the highest achievers today is to lead a personal and professional transformation for themselves and their teams. But that lofty goal can feel like attempting to change tires in the middle of rush-hour traffic. You have to lead transformation without sacrificing financial and operating results, or injuring your engagement scores.

So how exactly do you accomplish that? Here are four principles applied by some of the most successful (and most disruptive) leaders of the new world.

World Bank: Diversity and inclusion as a sustainable competitive advantage

As a physician, anthropologist, and Nobel laureate nominee, Jim Yong Kim was the first-ever nonfinancial executive to be appointed to lead the World Bank, which invests more than $700 billion in projects aimed at ending poverty around the globe. During his five years at the bank, Dr. Kim led a painful reinvention of the institution, reducing bureaucracy and waste, that resulted in a spectacular impact on programs: more than one billion fewer people now live below the poverty line.

In just one thirty-day stretch, the bank led over a dozen nations to raise $1.3 billion to support the largest women's entrepreneurship funding program in history. During my three years coaching the leadership team, I saw them change the world many times over, and the core asset driving their impact was their profound focus on diversity and inclusion. It's not just a matter of fairness and humanity—which are obviously crucial—it's an issue of brilliance.

Great leaders must ask: Where does your innovation come from? Are you tapping into a diverse collection of views and backgrounds or just one homogenous group of people? How do you touch and engage a diverse workforce and diverse customers in every community you serve?

The World Bank does it by welcoming, encouraging, and harvesting the eclectic, exotic, and entrepreneurial ideas and insights of a choir of more than eighty nations that fund the bank. It's not an imposition on management to hear out all these diverse ideas; it's not a separate HR "program" to be tolerated. It's a core asset, and the bank sees it as a crucial, sustainable competitive advantage. In fact, most countries send representatives to live onsite at the World Bank headquarters in Washington, DC. Imagine working *and* living with people whose cultures are different and come from every corner of the planet, but whose voices each contribute to the largest brain trust of financial minds ever to assemble on the globe? Diversity is power! It's the most natural source of differentiation from your competitors.

Virgin Group: Reinvent your assumptions, burn the house down

When Sir Richard's home burned, he had an epiphany about how to think about disruptive innovation that changed his life and work. He's long been one of history's greatest entrepreneurial innovators, launching more than 400 companies under the Virgin brand, touching almost every service business, from transportation to telecommunications, from health clubs to hotels. But his biggest insight about self-awareness and executive renewal in business came from losing his family home, the residence where he and his wife of three decades had raised their family (and now their grandchildren).

Think about what it would be like if your dream house went up in flames. Stop reading this article right now and consider that possibility seriously. Your house burned down. Feel that for a moment.

Okay, fortunately it didn't happen, but ask four important questions before the feeling wears off.

Would you:

- Rebuild your house exactly the same way, or would it be different?
- Recreate the same design, same architecture and space? Not likely.
- Restock it with all the same things? Probably not.
- Recruit all the same people to the project? If your organization vaporized, and your employees had all exited, would you work hard to invite certain people back to your organization? Who would that be? Would you not invite others back? If disaster struck, how would you decide what and who goes or stays? This can be a brutal and yet instructive set of lessons.

Why would you make all the above choices?

For Sir Richard, seeing his dream turn to ashes was a teachable moment of epic proportions—an unexpected provocation to rethink innovation in a world full of surprises. With 400 management teams in the Virgin group clamoring for growth, he now coaches them to be absolutely sure they're not just paving the old cow path unwittingly as they start construction or renovation. "Keep the best; lose the rest! If you think you don't have time to do this, then reimagine the inconvenience of having it all burn down. That would be a bigger bother!" he says.

Lyft: Values-driven leadership; nobody does it alone

Another critical principle shared by growth- and change-oriented leaders is to explicitly select a shared set of values around your mission. How will you establish collaborative behaviors in the workplace to grow your team and your organization?

Lyft cofounder Logan Green was inspired to start his company after a trip to Africa, where he was awestruck to observe extraordinarily cooperative mass transit in Zimbabwe, despite the apparent chaos of a developing country. People would swarm toward their destinations loaded with chickens and produce, and Green was aghast to see how everyone who needed a ride was encouraged to get a lift from an agreeable driver, whether perched on the roof of an overloaded bus or precariously clinging to the back of a motorbike. The shared mission of helping each other get somewhere is intrinsic to the Zimbabwean culture, creating an unprecedented level of collaborative transit.

The experience inspired Green to start ZimCar, a name he chose in honor of the African country rather than his cofounder's name, John Zimmer. Version 2.0 of that vision is a company called Lyft, a fast-growing ride-sharing firm, whose focus on values-based service and collaborative leadership serves as ballast during this period of exponential growth and change. Those values are part of the reason Lyft is quickly overtaking Uber, whose ethical debacles tarnished a brand once destined to inherit world dominance.

Recognizing the value of Lyft's focus on treating people better and building a sustainable technology platform, Green and Zimmer won billions of dollars of support from disruptive investors like Andreessen Horowitz, KKR, auto giant GM, and even Didi Kuaidi, Uber's chief rival in China. As part of a shared vision for safer, autonomous vehicles, Google is writing a big check to Lyft after investing early in Uber. (Google is also suing Uber for stealing technology.)

The lesson here is that values matter more than at any other time in organizational development history. Values-driven principles are not an idealistic luxury or a marginal choice. Management must sponsor leadership programs that empower teams to engage in professional development that helps everyone—from the CEO to the frontline employee—to change and grow in ethical ways that anchor their company to a customer-focused mission in the face of ridiculously challenging business conditions.

Pinterest: Redefining success

The fourth transformational principle embraced by the world's growth-company leaders relates to how you measure and manage meaning in your life and work. Pinterest founders Evan Sharp and Ben Silbermann envisioned a world where every individual could discover and activate their passions online—the world's biggest catalog of ideas to help people identify and actualize their desires.

Pinterest today engages more than 200 million users, and this fall reached a pre-IPO market value of over $12 billion. If you haven't paid the site a visit, it's time that you give yourself permission to explore what success means to you, because that's part of the secret formula that will help you generate sustainable success in a world characterized by dizzying change.

Disruptively successful people don't settle on just one definition of success, but engage in a lifelong struggle to balance each of the three in their decision-making, often describing it like juggling precious crystal balls while riding a unicycle. When you get them in sync, the result is something we all dream about in a world spinning with change: success that matters and lasts a lifetime.

Mark Thompson is a *New York Times* best-selling leadership author and America's No. 1 executive coach for growth companies. For a free copy of the World Success Survey, email Thompson at Mark@MarkCThompson.com.

TRIVIAL PURSUITS

Sudhir Venkatesh

A colleague recently launched a survey of American consumers. His research team wanted to know: how is coronavirus transforming Americans' consumer behavior? Some of the results affirmed their hypotheses. Consumers reported going online with greater ferocity; many were cautious about excessive spending; some were halting all nonessential consumption to protect their cash reserves.

One trend caught the research team by surprise. People were looking online for goods and services that they would never consider purchasing beforehand. Why? The most common response was that they wanted new experiences.

To understand this dynamic, the researchers called some respondents for deeper insight. In phone conservations, they learned that, although people felt socially distant and stuck at home, consuming gave them a chance to explore. Some took up golf or running, others were learning to draw, still others signed up for screenwriting or voice lessons. Their lives had been halted, but people felt liberated and free to spend time and energy on pursuits that might otherwise seem trivial, selfish, or just unimportant relative to other priorities. Consumption was a way to fuel this exploration.

The people who fell in this category reported that their newfound interests were keeping them sane. They felt energized and inspired to be more creative with their time. (In case you are wondering, even parents whose days were now busy with work and childcare admitted to relishing their mini-adventures.)

The lesson for those who think about leadership and performance: make time to explore, pursue a new experience, and, if possible, put yourself in the position of student, novice, or beginner. Doing so will sharpen your ability to lead. Let's explore why.

Our days are busier and far more scheduled than ever. Calendars filled with endless back-to-back meetings and continuous stress leave us little time to breathe. Work is growing more complex as technology and global interchange speed up the pace of change. These conditions continually raise new challenges and place us in unforeseen circumstances. Leaders are confronting unfamiliar terrain where the tasks seem to escape the tried-and-true formulas that once garnered success.

Putting it differently, leaders must continually overcome a basic contradiction: what they relied upon in the past is never entirely helpful because future challenges require them to pivot and develop a new approach. This observation is hardly new. Management training has embraced the mantra that agility is a hallmark of successful leaders and teams. But where do we learn agility? How can we grow more adaptable? How can we become better at confronting newness? It is difficult enough to get through the workday and maintain our personal lives. Finding the time to extend our strengths and discover new ways of seeing and doing seems a tall order.

The present moment may offer us a chance to get out of this trap. We might use the age of coronavirus as an unexpected opportunity to discover how adaptive, resilient, and creative we are—and how we can become better at confronting what lurks around the corner.

We can take some direction from those consumers who, for want of a better phrase, are avidly seeking trivial pursuits. Taking up a hobby or a new leisure activity, where the consequences are less serious, has several benefits for leaders. First, leadership is premised on curiosity and openness to serendipity. As a sociologist, I do not think this is an innate behavior, but one that can be refined over time into a powerful tool. But it takes commitment, especially when much of our days have repeated and expected patterns. It takes practice to break apart routine and incorporate new rhythms into our lives.

To revive this thirst for curiosity, reaching out and exploring new opportunities—whatever the size and scope—is a great place to start. Doing so creates valuable space for surprise. By definition, taking on an unfamiliar task will increase the possibility of new feelings, unpredicted happenings, unforeseen interactions with others, and so on.

At its core, allowing yourself to be surprised means you are open to the loss of control. This is not an easy skill to cultivate. The demands of work and family create pressures that require us to be in control—nearly all the time, as others are depending on it. Yet the teams we lead require leaders who are comfortable delegating power and authority, and who can accept the consequences that come with a loss of control. Who wants to work for a dictator?

Will taking up a new hobby or craft while sheltering in place help a person delegate authority more effectively at work? Probably not. But the germ of both is the same: becoming more comfortable performing in new situations where one may not possess the necessary expertise.

A continuous challenge for all leaders is to create reasonable expectations of success—for themselves and their teams. One obstacle may be found in the work process of most complex organizations. Before any collective activity, most leaders will spend vast amounts of time identifying the criteria for gauging team performance. It is now sacrosanct to identify metrics of success before dedicating time and energy to an activity. The problem with this approach is that it prioritizes efficiency over creativity. Metrics, by their very nature, are a form of control. They help leaders to differentiate signal from noise. But the risk is that we *a priori* decide what is unworthy of our attention ("noise").

Let's go back to our trivial pursuits. What is the metric of success of enrolling in an online drawing class or purchasing a new mountain bike? Part of the enjoyment and motivation is to be surprised by the outcome. Given that immediate expertise is not likely, the process must provide some enjoyment.

The drive to define key metrics and objectives and key results has made us less scrappy and less open to new circumstances. Sticking too closely with predetermined indicators and metrics can be a crutch, making it difficult to embrace unanticipated experiences that might generate new opportunities and insights. Openness to this form of discovery must be practiced. It means learning to have faith that one's labor will yield benefits even if the outcomes may not be spelled out in advance.

Here's to trivial pursuits!

Sudhir Venkatesh is William B. Ransford Professor of Sociology and director of the Tech Society Interface Lab at Columbia University. He has spent the past five years managing product teams for several large social media companies.

LEADING IN THE DARK

Liz Wiseman

The need to lead your team through change is nothing new. But we are now leading in a world of perpetual complexity, where you don't *move through* uncertainty, you *live in* uncertainty. Gone are the days where a leader's job was to determine a destination and then inspire their teams to journey with them to a "better place." Today's managers must lead their teams into the unknown, leaving the comfort of the status quo, under the dark of night, equipped with strategies that look more like a slice of Swiss cheese than a precise battle plan.

Middle managers know that too many unknowns create unrest and anxiety in the troops. When change is looming, it is too easy for managers to fall into the trap of waiting for new information to relay to their teams. They reason: *Next week I'll know more. We'll get more clarity after next month's exec meeting.* Meanwhile, the memo intended to communicate to their team just sits in their "drafts" folder. When managers go radio silent, employees not only fear the worst but begin to wonder if there is a leadership vacuum in the organization.

Rather than waiting for information or pretending you've got it figured out, let your people know what you don't know. You see, in fast times, everyone is winging it—even the leaders at the top. Perhaps the bravest act of leadership is to admit what you don't know.

I was working at Oracle during a time of rapid growth, massive change, and upheaval in the industry. I was the head of learning for the company and was meeting with three of the top executives to review feedback from a recent strategy forum and leadership training session. The feedback wasn't good: the participants felt like the strategy articulated by the top executives just wasn't clear. While I reviewed the feedback, the executives were unusually quiet. Assuming they didn't understand the participants' perspective, I reiterated the problem. Jeff Henley, the CFO (and my boss's boss), became agitated and blurted out, "Liz, you don't need to beat us up. We know we need to fix this. The problem is that we don't know how to do it." He motioned to his two colleagues, both senior executives whom I held in great esteem, and explained matter-of-factly, "We've never run a $25 billion company before, so this is new to us." The president and the CTO nodded in concurrence. I went slack-jawed. Henley continued, "If you could help us learn how to do this, that would be useful."

So I arranged for these executives to work with a renowned strategy guru, and we rearchitected the strategy, clarifying the core tenets (what was known) and laying out a set of questions (the unknowns). The senior executives then invited the managers below them to help find answers. Through this process we built something more valuable than a strategic plan; we built real-time strategic agility and a deep belief that we could navigate complexity.

We know that in an increasingly complex world, it isn't possible for us as leaders to have all the answers. However, we do need to be asking the right questions.

One of the best leaders I've seen was a physician leader in an academic hospital who led his team of residents through emergency and trauma situations daily. One of the residents reflected, "He clearly stated the limitations of what he and the team knew of the situation, and then he focused on the data we needed to gather." This leader's questions were direct and pointed, which helped his team of resident physicians focus and amid the chaos. He resident reflected, "Like a master teacher, he took me to the threshold of my own understanding and then helped me find the next logical position and take a step."

Here are four tactics that can help you and your team navigate complexity and find answers.

1. Identify what you do know.

Clarify what is known and the core assumptions at play. This will both build a collective understand and the confidence needed to move into the unknown.

2. Make a 'we don't know' list

Make a list of things you don't know but will need to better understand. Such a list will force you to get out of your own bubble and take a critical look at what is going on around you. Like the old saying, if you don't admit you have a problem, you'll never find a solution.

3. State the questions

Define the questions and the data needed to answer those questions well. A good question is one that focuses the team on the right problems and opportunities and invites (if not demands) novel thinking and new solutions.

4. Engage your team

Start by sharing with your team what you know, and then admit what you don't. Then let your team help you (and senior management) find answers. Nothing combats stress like putting people in charge of their fate. And don't limit this exercise to your immediate team; Share your list with your collaborators, brief them on your learning mission, and invite them to join you to navigate the uncertainty and find answers.

In times of flux, take charge—even if taking charge just means boldly letting people know what you don't know. When you stop waiting for answers to trickle down, you'll get new ideas bubbling up. And, in a world of perpetual complexity, you'll need all the intel you can get.

Liz Wiseman is a researcher and *New York Times* best-selling author who teaches leadership around the world. She is the author of three books: *Multipliers*, *The Multiplier Effect*, and *Rookie Smarts*. Wiseman has been listed on the Thinkers50 ranking and recognized as the top leadership thinker in 2019.

Made in the USA
San Bernardino, CA
02 June 2020